The United Kingdom's Journeys into and out of the European Union

This Routledge Focus explores the United Kingdom's relationship with the European Communities (EC) and the European Union (EU). Since joining the EC in 1973, the UK has had a fraught relationship with its European partners, declining closer economic union in the eurozone and often arguing against closer political union. While some 67% of the UK's voters opted to remain in the EC in a referendum held in 1975, by June 2016 a narrow majority voted to leave the EU. This volume examines the UK's journey into the Unionits difficulties within the Union and the fateful second referendum, arguing that the decision to leave in many ways reflected the reasons the UK had remained aloof in the first place. It then examines how the country's voters came to decide on Brexit and where the UK's departure from the EU may lead it.

Julie Smith is Director of the European Centre, POLIS Department, Cambridge University, and Fellow of Robinson College, Cambridge. She is also a member of the United Kingdom House of Lords.

Europa EU Perspectives: Reform, Renegotiation, Reshaping

Since their inception, the European Communities and, later, the European Union (EU) have undergone significant changes, some of which have proved to be controversial, demonstrating the policy differences between those believing in ever-closer political and economic union and those who favour a trade agreement only. The EU's ultimate aims have been raised and discussed many times during its history, and the referendum held in the United Kingdom on 23 June 2016 , at which a slim majority voted to leave the EU, may prove to mark a watershed in the organization's continuing development. This series aims to analyse the EU's previous and possible future reforms, the negotiations and renegotiations that have significantly affected and changed the organization, and the reshaping of the EU in the aftermath of the eurozone and refugee crises and the Brexit referendum.

Julie Smith is Director of the European Centre, POLIS Department, Cambridge University, and Fellow of Robinson College, Cambridge. She is also a member of the United Kingdom House of Lords.

The United Kingdom's Journeys into and out of the European Union
Destinations Unknown
Julie Smith

The United Kingdom's Journeys into and out of the European Union
Destinations Unknown

Julie Smith

LONDON AND NEW YORK

First published 2017
by Routledge
2 Park Square, Milton Park, Abingdon, Oxon OX14 4RN
and by Routledge
711 Third Avenue, New York, NY 10017

First issued in paperback 2018

Routledge is an imprint of the Taylor & Francis Group, an informa business

© 2017 Julie Smith

The right of Julie Smith to be identified as the author of the material has been asserted in accordance with sections 77 and 78 of the Copyright, Designs and Patents Act 1988.

All rights reserved. No part of this book may be reprinted or reproduced or utilised in any form or by any electronic, mechanical, or other means, now known or hereafter invented, including photocopying and recording, or in any information storage or retrieval system, without permission in writing from the publishers.

Trademark notice: Product or corporate names may be trademarks or registered trademarks, and are used only for identification and explanation without intent to infringe.

Europa Commissioning Editor: Cathy Hartley
Editorial Assistant: Eleanor Simmons

British Library Cataloguing in Publication Data
A catalogue record for this book is available from the British Library

Library of Congress Cataloging in Publication Data
A catalog record for this book has been requested

ISBN 13: 978-1-85743-972-4 (pbk)
ISBN 13: 978-1-85743-908-3 (hbk)

Typeset in Times New Roman
by Taylor & Francis Books

Contents

Acknowledgements		vi
Abbreviations		vii
1	Introduction	1
2	The Origins of European Integration: Emerging lines of (dis-)engagement	7
3	Winning and Losing: Money, power and the politics of treaty reform	25
4	Leaving the People Behind	43
5	Seeking to Reconcile Conservatives and Coalition	57
6	Cameron's Three Rs: Reform, renegotiation, referendum	76
7	Where do we Go from Here?	99
8	Postscript	112
	References	113
	Index	119

Acknowledgements

This book is the product of years of researching, living and breathing the EU and the UK's relations with it. Thus there are far too many people whose thoughts have fed into my own thinking over the years to be able to mention everyone by name.

Some of the thinking goes back to a History Special Subject on the European Integration process which I taught with Geoffrey Edwards when I first arrived in Cambridge, more years ago than I care to recall. Students for that paper, and many others over the years, have heard me outline and refine some of the arguments put forward in this book, and I am grateful to them for thoughts and ideas in mutually beneficial discussions.

I am especially grateful to everyone who agreed to be interviewed either specifically for this book or for a series of related projects. The insights of numerous politicians, advisers and the odd journalist going beyond what they may have already written in their personal memoirs or news columns have been invaluable in. I benefited from the views of colleagues in the House of Lords during the passage of the EU Referendum Act 2015 and beyond – some of which I agreed with, some of which I wholeheartedly disagreed with, but which were unerringly interesting and generally well-informed.

I am indebted to Geoffrey Edwards, Mark Field MP, James Gray MP, David Yates and William Wallace (Lord Wallace of Saltaire) for reading various drafts of the book, in some cases more than once. Inevitably any errors or omissions are my own.

Finally, my thanks go to Cathy Hartley of Routledge for her unfailing patience and support in ensuring that this book was commissioned and has finally made it to print.

Julie Smith
Cambridge, November 2016

Abbreviations

CAP	Common Agricultural Policy
CEE	Central and Eastern Europe/European
CJEU	Court of Justice of the EU
EC	European Communities
ECSC	European Coal and Steel Community
ECJ	European Court of Justice
EEC	European Economic Community
EFTA	European Free Trade Association
EMU	Economic and Monetary Union
EP	European Parliament
EPC	European Political Co-operation
EPP	European People's Party
ERM	Exchange Rate Mechanism
EU	European Union
Euratom	European Atomic Energy Community
FCO	Foreign and Commonwealth Office
GNI	gross national income
IGC	Intergovernmental Conference
IMF	International Monetary Fund
MEP	Member of the European Parliament
MFF	Multiannual Financial Framework
MP	Member of Parliament
NATO	North Atlantic Treaty Organization
NHS	National Health Service
PM	Prime Minister
PMB	Private Members' Bill
QMV	qualified majority voting
SEA	Single European Act
SNP	Scottish National Party
TEU	Treaty on European Union
UK	United Kingdom
UKIP	UK Independence Party
UN	United Nations
VAT	value added tax

1 Introduction

'Brexit means Brexit'

So announced incoming Prime Minister (PM) Theresa May in July 2016, on taking office in the wake of one of the most dramatic cases of self-inflicted prime ministerial damage ever seen in the United Kingdom. Her predecessor David Cameron's decision to hold a referendum on the UK's membership of the European Union (EU) was intended as a means to hold together a party long divided on an issue that was not politically salient for the vast majority of citizens, even if few people actively embraced the 'European project'. The referendum was not required constitutionally and few outside the Eurosceptic media and political class were actively calling for one. Yet Cameron believed he needed to resolve the matter in the interests of party management. He hoped to negotiate changes to the UK's terms of membership to enable him both to unite his party and to persuade a reluctant electorate to commit to staying in the EU. However, as leading figures, such as Secretary of State for Justice Michael Gove (whom Cameron reportedly considered a friend) and outgoing Mayor of London Boris Johnson, pledged to support the campaign to leave the EU, Cameron's chances of success receded. He gambled and lost. So too did Johnson. Both men assumed that the British public would vote to remain in the EU. For Cameron this would have meant securing his legacy, holding his party and country together, and keeping the UK in the EU. For Johnson the ideal was surely a narrow defeat for the 'Vote Leave' campaign – but with a sufficiently close result that he could claim that he had done great things for a campaign that started very much as the underdog yet which resonated with many of the Conservative Party faithful, thereby strengthening his own claims to the Party leadership when Cameron stepped (or was pushed) aside. The vote to leave left both men – and the country – without a clear strategy. The Government had laid no plans for a Leave vote, while those advocating an exit from the EU had failed to provide a blueprint for what the alternative arrangements might include.

Precisely what 'Brexit' meant was uncertain, despite the heated referendum campaign that preceded the June 2016 poll and followed forty years of pressure from Eurosceptics. May's words were designed to reassure those in her own party and beyond who were concerned that a PM who had supported remaining in the EU might not be wholly committed to taking the UK out of the Union: however they did little to clarify what the UK's future relationship with the EU might look like. The days and weeks immediately after the referendum were characterised by disbelief among many 'Remainers', millions of whom sought to have the outcome of the referendum overturned or simply ignored, with some arguing that the referendum result was not binding and others asserting that voters had been misled by lies put forward by those who advocated leaving. It was thus important for May to demonstrate that for her, as for Cameron, the decision **was** binding; the Conservatives had committed to accepting the outcome of the referendum in their 2015 manifesto. Nonetheless she required some time to begin to determine the UK's negotiating objectives prior to launching formal negotiations to leave the EU under the Article 50 provisions introduced in the Lisbon Treaty: she undertook to do this by the end of March 2017.

The departure of a member state from the EU is unprecedented, so Article 50 has never previously been invoked. The other 27 member states and the EU institutions, notably the European Parliament (EP) and the European Commission, have no more experience of negotiating the withdrawal of a member state than the UK has of leaving. While lawyers sought to make a wide range of claims about what might or might not be legal either within the UK or at the EU level, they typically forgot one crucial point: the decision to hold a referendum and the commitment of both Cameron and his successor to be bound by the results were not matters of law but of politics. That the referendum was not legally binding, in that neither the Government nor Parliament was formally required to accept an outcome unacceptable to the majority of parliamentarians, was beside the point. In committing to hold a referendum Cameron had bound himself and his party to the result; in their endorsement of the legislation, parliamentarians from across both houses had effectively, if unintentionally, made the same commitment. In the House of Lords there was a clear recognition that the referendum formed part of a Conservative manifesto pledge. Peers, cognisant of the Salisbury Convention, thus knew that it was not their place to try to thwart the will of Government to hold a referendum.[1] In the Commons, only the Scottish National Party (SNP) members of parliament (MPs) voted against the European Union Referendum Act 2015. Thus, as Cameron pointed out in his Commons statement following the Leave vote, 'Members on both sides of the House voted for a referendum by a margin of six to one' (HC Deb 27 June 2016, Col. 22). Hence, he was 'clear – and the Cabinet agreed this morning – that the decision must be accepted, and the process of implementing the decision in the best possible way must now begin' (HC Deb 27 June 2016, Col. 22).

Precisely how Cameron envisaged implementing the decision may never be known. In office he had undertaken to trigger Article 50 immediately in the event of a vote to leave the EU. When the unwelcome result emerged he quickly tendered his resignation as Conservative Party leader, arguing that the process of leaving the EU should be left to his successor. The prospect of a long summer given over to a Conservative Party leadership election battle beckoned, and with it the likelihood that any decisions on the UK's future relations with the EU would be put on hold. The dramatic events that led to the coronation without election by the party faithful of Theresa May as Conservative Party leader – and hence as PM – ensured that the prospective period of uncertainty was curtailed. Yet, as Chapter 7 makes clear, neither the new PM nor her ministers had a vision of the optimal relationship between the UK and the rest of the EU when they took office. Nor did they know what they would be able to negotiate with their erstwhile partners. It would be a journey into the unknown, just as nearly half a century earlier the UK found itself on the brink of a journey to an 'unknown destination' (Shonfield 1973), as it prepared to join the European Economic Community (EEC) or 'Common Market'.

Aim of this Volume

The aim of this book is to show how and why the UK has had such strained relations with the EU, culminating in the referendum decision to leave. It argues that many of the reasons why the UK stood aside in the early years of integration, such as concerns over sovereignty, the UK's role in the world and its commitment to free trade, also explain its subsequent 'awkwardness' (George 1998), for example over treaty reform, and its eventual decision to leave the EU. These core issues were compounded by the UK's own decisions and actions both before and after acceding to the European Communities. By joining late, the

UK was unable astutely to shape the institutions to suit itself or its own interests, as founding member states, notably France, had done. This would cause problems in the areas of budgetary contributions, the commitment to economic and monetary union (EMU) and questions of sovereignty. Moves towards the single market and enlargement, both of which were actively supported by the UK (under Margaret Thatcher and Tony Blair respectively, although for various reasons all PMs tended to favour enlargement) had knock-on consequences that would lead to significant hostility, as the UK lost sovereignty in an increasing number of policy areas and the final say over who could live and work in the UK. These issues would all contribute to the case made by those calling for the UK to leave the EU. All of them would still be at stake when it came to negotiating 'Brexit'.

Through analysis of key episodes in the UK's relationship with the EU, the book will show how the UK reached the position where its citizens voted to leave before being told of the issues that would face the UK and the EU following that decision – particularly regarding post-Brexit relations with the remaining EU and its members. Its focus is on the political aspects of the EU and the schisms it has caused in both main parties in the half-century since the UK initially sought membership. The constraints of space mean that no attempt is made to give all the details of events. It would be foolish even to try, although the extensive list of references gives some indications for further reading. Nor is a detailed economic analysis provided, though note is taken of the importance of economic factors in helping shape both the UK's relations with the EU and popular reactions to the EU. Moreover, while the media clearly coloured the context of political debate and helped shape public opinion over the years, the volume does not seek to assess the impact of the media on public opinion or their effect on the outcome of the referendum. Although these matters are hugely important, the aim here is to consider the nature of the EU and the choices that the UK has made, and how they have in turn shaped the relationship: the role of the media must remain for another volume.

The engagement (or otherwise) of British political parties is a key focus. Intraparty differences have rendered it difficult for politicians to address 'Europe' over the years, thereby creating difficulties for the 'Remain' campaign. For years, parties were reluctant to engage with the issue for fear of losing votes and provoking party splits. Thus there was little scope for citizens to express **their** views on the EU. Until the creation of the UK Independence Party (UKIP) in the 1990s, parties typically found it expedient to downplay European politics. Even the most consistently pro-EU party, the Liberal Democrats, tended to focus more on domestic politics, believing there were few votes to be won on Europe. For UKIP, the EU was the natural focus of activity and, alongside a significant swathe of Conservative activists and MPs who ignored the party line that the UK was better off in the EU, the party campaigned for years on an anti-EU ticket, effectively shifting the public agenda while pro-Europeans sat back, incorrectly assuming that the UK's place in the EU was secure. Coupled with burgeoning Eurosceptic press coverage, the relative activism of the two sides made it hard for those seeking to remain in the EU to overturn four decades of scepticism. The legacy of complacency that had characterised pro-Europeans would prove difficult to overcome in the course of a short referendum campaign. Correcting decades of inaccurate information about the EU would prove too great a challenge for the Remain side. Nor were the largest parties wholly committed to the Remain cause: the Conservatives were formally neutral, even if the Government was officially in favour of remaining, while Labour's contribution to the referendum seemed lacklustre, with much criticism of the formerly Eurosceptic leader Jeremy Corbyn's apparent lack of engagement.

Several themes, aside from party divisions, recur in the UK's relations with her European neighbours, from the 1950s when the Communities first came into being, through accession, and renegotiation and referendum (twice). Issues of national sovereignty, the EU's defects such as the 'democratic deficit', the British contributions to European coffers and relations with third countries (especially the Commonwealth) all played a part in the thinking of those who opposed membership. Advocates of membership focused predominantly on bread-and-butter issues throughout, even if some such as Edward Heath were driven by the same peace narrative as the founding fathers – the dream of making war among European states materially impossible. Many of the key issues underpinning the 2016 Leave campaign could be traced back to the initial concerns about joining the embryonic integration process, and to key decisions on the development of the EU in the intervening years. Frequently the latter had arisen from decisions where the UK was at the forefront, including the 1986 Single European Act (SEA) and the 2004 'big bang enlargement' that saw eight Central and Eastern European (CEE) states join the Union, enjoying rights of free movement that would lead to a backlash against European integration more generally a decade on.

The reasons for Leave reflected long-standing, if in some ways rather abstract, concerns over control or 'sovereignty', as well as economic concerns. They also underpin the Brexit conundrum as the UK tries to find its way out of the EU: how to regain control and yet remain in the single market, two competing goals of many regarding the EU. The choice would ultimately come down to politics versus economics. The drivers of Euroscepticism and calls to leave the EU are reminiscent of the reasons Baker et al. identified for opposition to the Maastricht Treaty in the early 1990s and highlight deep, ongoing divisions among sceptics and opponents of integration:

> Far from being an ideologically coherent group, some rejected Europe in favour of some vision of Anglo-Saxon independence and power; others rebelled against the loss of legislative sovereignty from Westminster; others were more specifically concerned at the loss of independent monetary policy-making implied by economic and monetary union. Despite the variety of their objections, the rebels were united in regarding the notion of irrevocability in the treaty as setting it apart from previous developments.
>
> (Baker et al. 1994, p. 46)

Yet if rebels, sceptics and Leavers all had different reasons for the positions they held, they nonetheless managed to make common cause (Baker et al. 1994). In 2015/16 they similarly managed to create a clear, unified message that would resonate with voters whatever their objections to the EU might be: 'Vote leave; take back control', they implored to great effect. This could have referred to control of taxes, laws, borders or trade. It was clear and concise and it appealed to both heart and head for many voters. By contrast the message of the Remain campaign, Britain Stronger in Europe, appealed – to the extent that it appealed at all – only to the head. Its relentless focus on pocket-book economics did not resonate with the majority of voters and thus gained little traction.

Note

1 Under the Salisbury Convention, peers do not vote against legislative proposals flagged up in the governing party's manifesto, although they may seek to amend specific aspects of the proposals.

2 The Origins of European Integration
Emerging lines of (dis-)engagement

The process of European integration that emerged in the 1950s in the form of the European Communities (EC) arose out of a need to rebuild European economies ravaged by war and a desire to end the possibility of war among European states. British politicians were initially reluctant to be involved in the three Communities established by France, Germany, Italy and the Benelux. During the 1960s, however, first the Conservatives and then Labour sought to take the UK 'into Europe' for essentially pragmatic reasons. In 1973, the UK's only passionately pro-European Prime Minister, Edward Heath, finally took the UK into the EC. Yet, almost as soon as it joined, the UK appeared in Stephen George's words to be 'an awkward partner' (George 1998). Divisions within the Labour Party led Harold Wilson to pledge to renegotiate the UK's terms of membership and allow citizens to decide on whether to remain in the EC, creating the precedent of a national referendum. This chapter explores the reasons behind the UK's original reluctance to engage in the European project before analysing the debates surrounding entry, renegotiation and referendum that set the pattern for Britain's contested EU relations for the next forty years, even if the 1975 referendum was thought to have settled the question of Britain's membership permanently. Sovereignty, money, peace and security would be recurring themes in British debates as the EC evolved into the EU and repeated treaty changes fundamentally altered the UK's relations with its neighbours.

A European Peace Project

European integration began as a visionary way to secure peace in Europe in the wake of two world wars. Deploying economic means for political ends, the founding fathers hoped to make war among participating European states 'materially impossible'. States that had endured centuries of invasion and armed conflict began to look for ways to establish peaceful, stable and enduring relations. Divergent experiences during and immediately after the Second World War help explain the UK's ambivalent relationship with her European neighbours. This ambivalence would affect the UK's initial thinking on whether to co-operate with the emerging Communities, and has contributed to the UK's ongoing differences ever since. While leaders in other Western European states were willing to pool sovereignty in return for peace and prosperity, the UK was and remains reluctant to cede sovereignty. The UK emerged from World War Two as a victor, one of the very few European states to have been neither invaded nor defeated. Thus, while it recognised the importance of peaceful co-operation across the Channel, the predominant view was that outlined by wartime leader Winston Churchill, who told the House of Commons in 1953 that the UK was 'with' but not 'of' European endeavours to co-operate. It was fine, even desirable, for European states to come together but not for the UK to join them.

Security, economics and geopolitics were the drivers of integration as Western European nations sought to rebuild their states politically and economically. In the immediate aftermath of the war, there was a need 'to keep the Americans in, the Soviets out and the Germans down'; factors that contributed to the development of the North Atlantic Treaty Organization (NATO) and, more significantly regarding the German question at least, to moves to integrate 'Europe' (typically used as short-hand for Western Europe and the EC during the Cold War). At the time Germany was divided – a situation which suited its European neighbours, since a divided Germany was a weakened Germany, hence the oft-quoted words attributed to French author François Mauriac: 'I like Germany so much I'm glad there are two of her'. Binding the Federal Republic of Germany, or 'West Germany', into the democratic western sphere of influence was a European solution to the German question. The USA too recognised the importance of Europe, a buffer zone against the then Soviet Union, and hoped to reduce the likelihood of further European conflict of the sort which had dragged it from isolationism into two world wars. It thus sought to foster co-operation through Marshall Aid. While the overt aim of the money was to offer financial assistance to states devastated by war, there was a sub-text: to encourage European states to co-operate in order to reduce the likelihood that they would engage in further conflict necessitating US intervention. The money was thus made conditional on the European states finding a way to co-operate in disbursing the funds, the hope being that they would come together in a federal enterprise modelled on the USA (Harper 1996). The UK was resistant to such ideas and the resulting Organization for European Economic Cooperation (OEEC) was resolutely intergovernmental.

A second attempt at peaceful unification of European states occurred in 1948 at the Congress of Europe in The Hague, which brought together passionate European federalists. The idealism of participants was best expressed by the former Belgian Prime Minister Paul Van Zeeland (1948, p. 22), who asserted that, 'This Congress has a mission: it is to answer the prayer of the masses of Europe; to give more precise and more concrete expression to their aspirations; to show the governments that even if they are daring in conception, public opinion will follow them, if indeed it is not already ahead of them.' Such words, which sound hubristic in the light of public opinion across the EU in the second decade of the twenty-first century, resonated at the time with many politicians and academics who believed that there was indeed a groundswell of opinion seeking co-operation across borders. The idea of a 'permissive consensus' assuming that where élites led the people would follow was thus born and would play a guiding role in the development of the European project for the next half century (see Wallace and Smith 1995).

Many of those present at the Congress of The Hague anticipated and indeed favoured what Hendrik Brugmans (1970) referred to as 'a parliamentary revolution, a "Saint Bartholomew's Night" of national sovereignties'. Such a cavalier attitude towards sovereignty would be anathema to many in the UK in the 21st century; nor was it universally acceptable in the 1940s. Thus, along with their Scandinavian counterparts, British participants at the Congress pressed for intergovernmental co-operation. The upshot was the creation of the intergovernmental Council of Europe, with its Court of Human Rights and Parliamentary Assembly located in Strasbourg. Formally entirely separate from what became the EU, the Council of Europe was important in two regards: firstly, the creation of a parliamentary assembly, which would create a precedent for the EU, and secondly for its focus on human rights – over the years, membership of the Council of Europe would become a proxy for meeting the human rights criteria for joining the EU.

Frustration about the British resistance to federalism inspired the French to seek another way forward. On 9 May 1950 French Foreign Minister Robert Schuman made his eponymous declaration, calling for France and Germany to come together to make war between their two countries 'materially impossible'. While the Schuman Declaration left open the prospect of other countries joining the Franco-German couple, the focus was on those two long-standing enemies. In that sense, it was wholly in line with Churchill's call for a United States of Europe and his proclamation in Zurich that, 'There can be no revival of Europe without a spiritually great France and a spiritually great

Germany' (Churchill 1946, p. 8). Of course, Churchill was out of office at the time of his Zurich speech and the Labour Government was not won over to the idea of European co-operation as envisaged by Schuman and by the driving force behind his Declaration, the Head of the French *Commissariat au Plan*, Jean Monnet, a technocrat who would suffuse the European Communities with the sort of rational bureaucracy that characterised French administration.

That the Labour Government of the day should have been reluctant to engage in the French vision of European co-operation – the word integration arose somewhat later – was not surprising. Monnet's proposals were based on 'functional integration', namely the idea that if states began to co-operate in one policy or 'functional' area they would begin to build up mutual trust and increase the likelihood of co-operation in other functionally related areas. In this way, relations between states would improve. This would be strengthened further by the choice of coal and steel as the first commodities to be pooled. Neither was chosen by chance: steel was required for making weapons and coal was needed by the French to rebuild their industrial base – Germany had large reserves of coal in the Ruhr region. The visionary aspect of the proposal was that 'The common production thus established will make it plain that **any war between France and Germany becomes not only unthinkable, but materially impossible**' (Schuman Declaration; emphasis added). The added benefit for France was clearly economic.

For a British Labour government that had only recently nationalised coal and steel, the prospect of pooling reserves was far less attractive. Nor were Labour politicians of the day persuaded of the merits of pooling sovereignty. Having won the war, the UK could not see any need to throw its lot in with a set of countries that it had helped either liberate or defeat. Churchill's rather patrician support from the margins was reflective of the UK's approach from both sides of the political divide. Some hoped that Churchill's return to power in 1951 might see a shift in the UK's position towards engagement with the European countries soon known as 'the Six', but they were to be disappointed. His focus was on three spheres of influence – the USA, the Commonwealth and Europe – with Europe the least important. The UK still had a global role and global ambitions, despite its loss of Empire through decolonisation and the emergence of the Commonwealth. More crucial was the bilateral transatlantic relationship with the USA – a centrepiece of foreign policy for the UK even if Americans tended to place less emphasis on it. Certainly the UK could not see the need for a new European order to give it a self-confident place in the world, in contrast to France, which would use Europe as a proxy for its declining global reach in unspoken recognition of its diminished international role. Indeed, agreeing to be a partner of France and Germany would have indicated a step away from such global ambitions.

Thus the Treaty of Paris establishing the European Coal and Steel Community (ECSC), signed on 18 April 1951, brought together just six Western European countries: France, Germany, Italy and the three Benelux countries. Each of the Six anticipated certain benefits from the new arrangements: for Germany and Italy they would pave the way for post-war rehabilitation, allowing them to regain political legitimacy; for the Benelux countries they would enhance security against their two largest neighbours; and for France there were dual benefits of security and prosperity. Indeed these factors were enshrined in the Schuman Declaration, the political goals of which were clear:

> In this way there will be realized simply and speedily that fusion of interests which is indispensable to the establishment of a common economic system; it may be the leaven from which may grow a wider and deeper community between countries long opposed to one another by sanguinary divisions. [...] this proposal will lead to the realization of the first concrete foundation of a European Federation indispensable to the preservation of peace.
> (Schuman Declaration, reprinted in Salmon and Nicol 1997, p. 45)

The language of the Treaty of Paris was similar, noting that the signatory states had 'resolved to substitute for age-old rivalries the merging of their essential interests; to create by establishing an economic community, the basis for a broader and deeper community among peoples long divided by bloody conflicts; and to lay the foundations for institutions which will give direction to a destiny henceforward shared, [...]' (reprinted in Salmon and Nicol 1997, p. 48).

The overtly political aspects of the ECSC, coupled with the fact that the French wanted it to commit to 'supranationalism' even before it was clear what that concept meant, ensured that the UK played no part in the ECSC or in moves to create a European Defence Community (EDC) and associated federal European Political Community. Creating a federation which entailed the loss of sovereignty was not on the British agenda. By contrast, when the EDC plans collapsed in the French National Assembly in 1954, the UK under Anthony Eden did take a lead in establishing Western European Union (WEU), an intergovernmental body that reflected the UK's willingness to engage in pragmatic co-operation with European neighbours. Yet when Monnet and others sought to restart the process of European integration with proposals for an Atomic Energy Community and a much wider-ranging Economic Community, the UK again refused to participate.

The Atomic Energy Community could be seen as a logical corollary to the Coal and Steel Community, as nuclear power has both civilian and military uses. The Economic Community, meanwhile, was intended to offer a broader canvas for integration. The UK felt that in light of the collapse of EDC the new Economic Community was unlikely to succeed and in a reflection of its attitudes to the European project sent only a mid-ranking civil servant to observe the 1955 negotiations at Messina where the Six were hoping to 'relaunch Europe'; other states sent their foreign ministers (see Young 1998). British reluctance to join the emerging process of integration would ensure that the rules of the game were set to suit other countries, notably France. By the time the UK sought membership and finally joined the Communities, it found itself facing arrangements that would suit neither its political nor economic interests as well as they did those of the founder members. Nor would those founding states be minded to reform in ways that would suit the UK, which had remained aloof at the outset when it had had the chance to participate and help shape the emerging enterprise.

Emerging Supranationalism – the European Institutions

The institutional arrangements for the ECSC (and subsequently Euratom and the EEC) drew their inspiration from French administrative patterns but in a unique form for inter-state relations. In particular, the High Authority of the ECSC was based on the Saint-Simonian concept of enlightened rational bureaucracy (or 'technocracy'), which underpinned administration in France. As states prepared to cede sovereignty in the limited fields of coal and steel, so decisions would be taken by the executive High Authority comprising appointees from each member state who enjoyed delegated authority, not as representatives of those member states but as a supranational European-level institution. A parliamentary body, the Common Assembly, was established to have oversight over the High Authority in light of the powers that had been ceded to it. With the establishment of the Economic and Atomic Energy Communities under the two Treaties of Rome in 1957, the High Authority was complemented by two European Commissions, which were to serve as the executive bodies for the new Communities. From 1967 the three executive bodies were merged into one European Commission, whose multifaceted roles included serving as 'guardian of the treaties', the initiator of legislation and the executive body required to oversee its implementation. The Common Assembly was expanded and renamed the European Parliamentary Assembly. (In 1962 it began to refer to itself as the European Parliament [EP], a title it formally acquired in the 1980s via the SEA.) Yet the Assembly remained a weak institution, denuded of any serious legislative power in the early years when its role was simply 'advisory and supervisory' and composed of representatives from national parliaments rather than directly elected. The benefits of the connection between national and European levels of this 'democratic figleaf' were offset by a sense that the Assembly was not truly representative, that the Community was not democratic and that there was a lack of adequate democratic accountability of the technocracy that was the Commission; a legacy that persisted to 2016 even though by that time the EP had acquired considerable powers and been directly elected for nearly 40 years.

The High Authority/Commission and the Assembly were both intended as supranational institutions, reflecting in the case of the Commission the 'European interest' to the extent that such a thing could be discerned (Commissioners were banned from taking a national line in their work, even though they relied on their member state to secure nomination in the first place) and in the case of the Assembly, the 'peoples' of the member states. At the behest of the Dutch, a Council of Ministers representing the member states was also established, which was intended to secure the rights of smaller members, although over time the Commission began to fulfil the role of protector of small member states while the Council seemed to bolster larger member states' interests. A European Court of Justice (ECJ) based in Luxembourg (not to be confused with the European Court of Human Rights based in Strasbourg) was established to oversee the implementation of the Treaty of Paris and later the two Treaties of Rome. Its jurisdiction was initially very limited, in line with the narrow sectoral competences (or 'powers') of the ECSC. Over the years its role became ever more significant as the Communities acquired more competences and as landmark rulings asserted that Community law was supreme over national law (Costa v ENEL, 1964) and that it had 'direct effect' on the citizens (Van Gend en Loos, 1963), quite unlike public international law whose effect was on states, not individual citizens. All this – the pooling of sovereignty, the supremacy of European law and the prospect of direct elections – was clear by the time the UK actively sought membership of the Communities, but its significance seems to have been conveniently ignored or pushed aside by politicians, media and, hence, the public at the time, contributing, alongside the expansion of the EU and the ECJ's sphere of influence over the subsequent forty years, to some of the concerns raised by Eurosceptics leading the charge for the UK to leave the EU in 2016.

The Treaty of Rome establishing the EEC 'acted as a spur to greater economic growth without a crippling loss of national autonomy, and was seen to be flexible enough to embrace both free marketeers and *dirigistes*. It did not provide for a common foreign policy or a political federation, retaining instead the obscure catch-all word, 'union' (Deighton 1995, p. xvi). At that time, the UK was looking for intra-European economic co-operation that did not entail a fundamental loss of sovereignty, its overriding concern being to be able to trade freely with other European states. An Economic Community predicated on free movement of goods, capital, services and labour, as envisaged in the Treaty of Rome, scarcely met with British approval and the UK thus set about creating the European Free Trade Association (EFTA). Bringing together seven sovereign countries on an intergovernmental basis, EFTA appeared to offer the UK everything it sought: economic co-operation without a political cost in terms of loss of sovereignty. Barely had the EEC come into being when British leaders began to reconsider their position. So began a period where the UK tried and failed to join the European project, as a result of which myriad transport metaphors were coined to the effect that the UK had missed the boat, train or bus. Having failed to board at the start of the journey, it would rapidly find the price of joining late would be costly, both financially and in terms of determining the ultimate destination.

An Early Application to Join

The Six always envisaged that integration would be open to other like-minded European states, and Article 237 of the original version of the Treaty of Rome states:

> Any European State may apply to become a member of the Community. It shall address its application to the Council, which shall act unanimously after obtaining the opinion of the Commission.
>
> The conditions of admission and the adjustments to this Treaty necessitated thereby shall be the subject of an agreement between the Member States and the applicant State. This agreement shall be submitted for ratification by all the Contracting States in accordance with their respective constitutional requirements.

In 1961, Conservative Prime Minister Harold Macmillan became the first leader to test this provision after a series of events caused a re-evaluation of the decision to stand aside. The 1956 Suez Crisis in particular had brought into question two of Churchill's spheres of influence – relations with the USA soured and the Commonwealth had proved unresponsive – and British foreign policy east of Suez was in tatters. Moreover, while the EEC members were enjoying economic success, the same could not be said of EFTA, which was dominated by the UK, as by far the largest member.

Macmillan's decision to apply came after a visit to the USA, during which President John F. Kennedy made clear America's support for British membership of the Community – the USA had long favoured British integration into Europe, yet the UK had persisted in believing that membership would in some way damage its transatlantic relations. For two years the UK explored the possibility of membership – not because of any new-found zeal for integration, and certainly not out of any desire to pool sovereignty, although Macmillan himself saw the merits of integration – but for pragmatic reasons associated with a re-evaluation of its position in the world. There were no clear rules outlined for the accession process and, anyway, on 14 January 1963, French President General Charles de Gaulle ended the UK's European ambitions at a press conference where he simply said, '*Non*': the UK could not join. De Gaulle appeared not to have consulted the Heads of Government of the other five member states, but since Article 237 required the Council to act by unanimity he did not need to: France could unilaterally block British membership of the Communities and had done so.

In many ways de Gaulle's decision was counter-productive given his intergovernmental approach to integration – having taken office in 1958, shortly after the Treaties of Rome had come into effect, De Gaulle's attitude to European integration was markedly different from those of Monnet and Schuman. While he supported French membership of the Community for the economic benefits it conferred, he firmly opposed the incremental federalism favoured by Monnet, believing instead in *une Europe des patries* (a 'Europe of [sovereign] nation states') in line with the prevailing British preferences (George 1991, p. 17). Yet, there was one crucial issue that divided the British and Gaullist positions. As Stephen George (1991, pp. 42–43) notes, the type of Europe the UK favoured was clear at the time of Messina: 'Politically it was a Europe of sovereign states, which would act together as a loyal ally of the United States. Economically it meant a Europe that would constitute a free-trade area without interventionist central policies, and open to commerce with the rest of the world' – a view that would persist into the twenty-first century. Loyalty to the USA would prove a stumbling block, as the French President feared the UK would prove to be an American 'Trojan horse'. Thus, he argued: 'It can be foreseen that the cohesion of its members, who would be very numerous and very diverse, would not endure for long, and that finally it would appear as a colossal Atlantic community under American domination and direction which would quickly have absorbed the European Community' (quoted in Salmon and Nicol 1997, p. 89). He was furthermore anxious to avoid any rival for supremacy in the emerging Community – with Germany divided, though growing economically, and Italy still struggling to build effective political institutions, France was the leading player in the Communities in 1963. A sovereign United Kingdom with global ambitions was liable to threaten France's pre-eminent position. As de Gaulle noted (de Gaulle 1963, pp. 132–3), 'The Treaty of Rome was concluded between six continental States, States which are, to put it briefly, economically of the same nature ... Furthermore, it happens that there exists between them no kind of political grievances, no border disputes, no rivalry for domination or power ... '

The difference between the other five member states and the UK was clear for all to see: only the UK stood to challenge France's leading role. Having rebuffed the UK, de Gaulle immediately pressed ahead with a bilateral agreement with Germany, the 'Franco-German Treaty on Friendship and Reconciliation', signed on 22 January 1963 and generally known as the Elysée Treaty, which paved the way for a strong, deep and heavily institutionalised relationship between these two countries. The strength of Franco-German relations would gradually transcend relations between their leaders, to include their respective parliaments and civil services. The UK would never be in a position to develop such close ties to other member states, which made it harder to find the allies it would need to be able to pursue its own interests successfully when it finally joined the Communities.

In 1967 it was Labour Prime Minister Harold Wilson who decided the UK's future lay within the EC. Ever the pragmatist, Wilson's move arose because of the UK's worsening economic situation at a time when the EEC was clearly outperforming EFTA and the Community was about to impose a common external tariff, which would have had a negative impact on the UK had it remained outside the Community (and which the UK is likely to see reimposed after withdrawing from the EU, unless a special deal is done). Wilson's move reflected a view newly prevailing in the Labour Party and shared by his Foreign Secretary, George Brown, and Secretary of State for Economic Affairs, Michael Stewart, namely that there was '*no alternative* for Britain, if she wished to remain an important power' (Young 1993, p. 95), rather than any real enthusiasm for the Community. Wilson thus stressed the economic benefits of membership, stating in a House of Commons statement on 2 May 1967 that: 'all of us are aware of the long-term potential for Europe, and, therefore, for Britain, of the creation of a single market of approaching 300 million people, with all the scope and incentive which this will provide for British industry, and of the enormous possibilities which an integrated strategy for technology, on a truly Continental scale, can create' (Wilson 1967).

Significantly, Wilson also stressed the political aspects of integration: ' ... the House will realise that, as I have repeatedly made clear, the Government's purpose derives, above all, from our recognition that Europe is now faced with the opportunity of a great move forward in political unity and that we can – and indeed must – play our full part in it' (Wilson 1967). What clearer rebuttal could there be for those who claim that the political ends of Community membership were hidden? However, despite Wilson's new-found enthusiasm for integration, this second British attempt was also rebuffed by de Gaulle, whose rationale on that occasion was that the EC should not accept a country coming cap-in-hand in the face of global changes alongside the UK's 'great economic, financial, monetary and social difficulties' (de Gaulle 1967, p. 157). The application was not withdrawn, but it remained on hold until de Gaulle left office.

The Hague Summit Changes the Game

De Gaulle's departure from the French political scene and his replacement as President in mid-1969 by Georges Pompidou finally allowed the Community to pay more serious attention to enlargement. Pompidou recognised that the Five had long favoured British membership – in the case of the Netherlands in particular to provide something of a counterweight against Franco-German dominance. By 1969 the *Ostpolitik* of Willy Brandt created a reason for Pompidou to support British membership, as it was expected to provide some ballast against a potential drift in West German policy at a time when the Cold War divisions of the continent appeared to have hardened. Yet if Pompidou was more willing than de Gaulle to countenance the expansion of the Community, it would not be at any price. Recognising that the UK had not suddenly espoused the sort of vision for European integration shared by the Six, Pompidou was determined to ensure that its accession would not weaken the integration process. It was thus determined by the Heads of State and Government of the Six, meeting in The Hague in December 1969, that any would-be member state would have to accept the full *acquis communautaire* – essentially, the sum total of the primary and secondary European legislation in place. Whereas founding member states could determine the rules of the game and existing members could block changes to those rules, newcomers would be offered membership on the terms prevailing at the time they joined. This principle remained an essential part of decisions on enlargement half a century later, ensuring that the later a country applied the higher the hurdles to joining it would face, and severely curtailing the prospects of a country like Turkey ever meeting the requisite standards.

In addition, Pompidou argued that before enlargement or 'widening' could occur, the Community needed to be 'completed', meaning that the Common Agricultural Policy (CAP), Common Fisheries Policy (CFP) and arrangements for the Community budget all needed to be finalised before the UK joined. 'Deepening' was also required, with the chosen areas for further integration being co-operation in foreign policy and the establishment of EMU, both envisaged by the end of the 1970s. While proposals for foreign policy co-operation, which came to be called European Political Co-operation (EPC), were outside the formal Community framework and as such clearly intergovernmental and, hence, acceptable to the UK, the proposals for EMU would entail a considerable loss of national sovereignty. At the time the UK sought membership there was nothing it could do to impede such proposals: if it was serious about joining it would be on the founding members' terms.

The UK en route to Europe

Negotiations for membership began under Wilson's Labour Government, although his party remained divided on the European question. The Conservative election victory in 1970 ensured that the negotiations were conducted under the premiership of Edward Heath, the UK's only truly committed pro-European PM (although Harold Macmillan also understood the European ideal and Tony Blair was a committed pro-European until relations with George W. Bush over the Iraq War led him to pivot towards the USA as all his predecessors apart from Heath had done). Heath's passion for the European project was redolent of that demonstrated by the founding fathers; he was not some pragmatic politician persuaded by narrow economic interests to support membership; he was a full-blown, passionate believer in the vision of a united Europe (see Heath 1998; Young 1998). Shaped by his time in continental Europe during and after the war, Heath believed it was vital for the UK to co-operate more closely with its nearest neighbours. Heath's personal convictions made negotiations with Pompidou easier than they might otherwise have been; at the time such bilateral discussions were rather more important than formal negotiations of the intricate type conducted by the European Commission for subsequent enlargements (or than that anticipated for the UK's 'reverse' negotiations under Article 50 in preparation for leaving the EU).

The terms of accession negotiated under the Conservative Party were very similar to those that Labour were negotiating when they lost office (see Thomson 1999). However, they were seen by some as suboptimal, as Heath was willing to cede ground on budgetary matters, for example, to secure what for him was the ultimate prize of British membership of the EEC. Labour, which in opposition had shifted to a far less 'pro-Market' stance,[1] was critical of the deal that had been secured, referring to 'Tory terms', even though they were indistinguishable from the terms that would have been agreed in the event of a Labour victory in 1970. Moreover, some in Heath's own party remained ambivalent or hostile to membership.

Once Heath had secured a deal with Pompidou, he had to get domestic approval for accession. Heath was determined that membership should be ratified by parliamentary means, not by referendum as was the case in the three other countries that sought to join alongside the UK – Norway, Ireland and Denmark. There was no precedent for direct democracy in the UK and Heath, while anxious to assert that he would take the views of the people into consideration, was adamant that the parliamentary route was the correct one. With hindsight, a popular vote to endorse membership might have averted some of the subsequent difficulties that arose from a lack of popular consent – or alternatively might, as in the case of Norway, have resulted in the UK not joining the Common Market. (Norwegians rejected membership in 1972 and again in 1994; the only citizens to do so when given the chance to vote, preferring to retain their national sovereignty, even if this was more illusory than real, given that membership of the European Economic Area would require them to follow the EU's rules without having 'a seat at the table'.) Yet at the time few in the UK would have argued that popular consent via a referendum was either necessary or desirable – the doctrine of representative democracy that prevailed across the political divide regarded referendums as the devices of dictators and demagogues.

In order to secure a majority for accession, Heath required support from some Labour MPs, given the divisions in his own party. Labour was also divided. However, there were sufficient pro-Market Labour MPs to help secure the bill, a feat achieved by a clever shadow whipping system organised by a young Labour MP, John Roper. On 17 October 1972 the European Communities Act was finally approved and the UK was set finally to join the European Communities, thanks largely to a Prime Minister who was passionate in his conviction that this was best for Britain and willing to make the case for it, both among the Six and in the UK. The very Act would over the years become a source of opprobrium for Conservative Eurosceptics, who would seek its repeal with ever more zeal.

On 1 January 1973, the Communities enlarged for the first time, taking in the UK along with its closest neighbour, Ireland, and Denmark. The latter joined, in effect, on the UK's economic coat-tails, having also been a member of EFTA. The Irish case was more complex. Having secured independence in 1922, the Republic sought to differentiate itself from the UK, yet the ties of history, geography and trade ensured that it remained deeply entwined with the former colonial power. Those links included a passport union, whereby Irish and British citizens could travel freely across the two states and which minimised issues of border controls between Northern Ireland and the Republic. Membership of the EC gave the Republic a new international status and brought economic benefits, allowing it to come out from the shadow of the UK. The Republic's membership of the EC (and later of the EU) was thus predicated on its relationship with the UK – a relationship that ensured that even after accession some of Ireland's European choices, such as over Schengen membership, were constrained by British reluctance to integrate. For the Republic, membership of the Community proved a liberating experience and it rapidly became one of the most pro-European members. For the UK meanwhile there was immediate antipathy, and early calls to look again at both the terms of membership and even at membership itself.

Renegotiation

In opposition, Labour's support for entering the Community had diminished, the views of the parliamentary rebels notwithstanding. By the time the Heath Government fell in February 1974, Labour was promising to renegotiate the 'Tory' terms of membership. The renegotiation would be followed by public endorsement, either through a second general election or an unprecedented referendum. By the second general election in October 1974, the party's position had hardened to one of a referendum. On re-election, Wilson despatched his Foreign Secretary, James Callaghan (like Wilson himself, at most a pragmatic pro-European) to negotiate with the other member states.

While the criticism of 'Tory terms' was perhaps unwarranted, the terms the UK had been given were not entirely favourable on a number of counts, particularly around the financial contributions the UK was expected to make. At the time of accession, the UK was seen as 'the sick man of Europe', ravaged by strikes, unemployment, inflation and soon requiring bailouts from the International Monetary Fund (IMF). Yet the way the Community budget had been conceived, the UK was required to make larger net contributions than other members. As a relatively more industrialised economy, the UK found itself making significant payments into the Community coffers, because of high value added tax (VAT) receipts. It received only limited payments from the Community budget, as one of the main items of expenditure was the CAP. The inspiration for the CAP was a perfectly laudable one: to ensure food security. In the wake of the Second World War Austria and Germany were on the verge of starvation. The CAP was intended to make the Community self-sufficient. As with many other aspects of integration, it played to the advantage of France, whose farmers stood to benefit from it much more than did British farmers; the system would prove more costly and less efficient than the traditional system of deficiency payments used in the UK – topping up farmers' incomes when prices were low, rather than artificially inflating prices to guarantee those incomes (and, of necessity, the food prices themselves). The upshot was a costly agricultural policy which would remain a source of contention in the UK right through to the 2016 membership referendum, despite numerous reforms over the years. Overall the UK was a large net contributor, which Wilson deemed unacceptable and set out to resolve.

Budgetary contributions were thus a key aspect of the UK's renegotiation in 1974–75, which resulted in a complex 'corrective mechanism', designed to resolve the worst excesses of the UK's budgetary payments. In practice, the mechanism was so complicated that it was destined never to be triggered. Years later, Helmut Schmidt, who as German Chancellor at the time had been particularly helpful to the UK, admitted that the renegotiation had essentially been window-dressing, which had changed little (Young 1998). Wilson deemed the deal that Callaghan negotiated for the UK sufficient for him to recommend to the Cabinet and then to the country that the UK should remain in the Common Market. For the first time in its history the UK would hold a referendum.

Referendum

Initially hostile to the idea of a referendum, Wilson was persuaded by left-wing Labour MP Tony Benn that it could be a way to hold the Labour Party together over an issue that cut across party lines, as proven by the parliamentary votes on the European Communities Act 1972. For Benn, the issue was a more fundamental one: sovereignty, as it was for then Conservative MP Enoch Powell on the right of the political spectrum and as it would be for many passionate Leavers of left and right forty years later. Benn had called for a referendum in 1971 because: ' ... the issue was of such major constitutional significance, because of the loss of sovereignty involved, that it should be put before the British electorate' (Benn cited in Smith 1999, note 27). While the British public was not particularly supportive of Community membership, accession had been achieved via the correct constitutional procedures and there was little sense of popular uprising against it – 'Europe' was an issue of low salience in the 1970s and would continue to be so throughout the UK's membership, despite the internal problems it created for Britain's political class. The decision to hold a referendum was all about holding together a divided party rather than a divided nation, as would be the case for David Cameron four decades later.

Yet, if membership was an issue of low salience, it was not a popular one, with public opinion polls consistently showing little popular support for membership (Butler and Kitzinger 1996, p. 247). The timing of the referendum proved fortuitous, however. Global food prices had risen dramatically before the referendum but the CAP ensured that European (and hence British) food prices remained stable. A focus on 'bread-and-butter' issues, notably food prices, was thus an effective way of securing a 'Yes' vote. While those hostile to the Community stressed the loss of sovereignty, as their successors would do in 2016, this carried little weight in 1975. The referendum offered a simple choice: 'Should the UK be a member of the European Economic Community (the "Common Market")?' Voters could indicate 'Yes' or 'No'.

The balance of campaign activity, resources and support from mainstream politicians, media and business were all heavily in favour of the 'Yes' campaign. The print media were solid in their support for membership, with the *Daily Star* the only daily in favour of leaving and *The Spectator*, a right-wing weekly, an outlier in its position – that the UK would be better outside the Community. Business leaders advocated staying in and put their money behind 'Britain in Europe' (BiE), the umbrella organisation of the 'Yes' campaign. BiE secured vastly more funding (£1,825,000) than the National Referendum Campaign (NRC), the umbrella 'No' grouping (£8,610), (Butler and Kitzinger 1996, pp. 86, 110). In addition, state funding of £125,000 was provided to each of the two umbrella organisations. The Government was firmly behind the 'Yes' campaign, producing a brochure (*'Britain's New Deal in Europe'*) for circulation to every household, which made a remarkably similar case to that outlined in the umbrella BiE campaign's '*Why you should vote YES*', even to the extent of including identical quotations from Commonwealth leaders. That the Commonwealth's opinion should matter reflected the ongoing significance of the Commonwealth to the UK's international position and the not insignificant issue of imports of New Zealand lamb and butter, which had been adversely affected by accession but improved thanks to the renegotiation (Smith 1999, p. 53).

With the support of the political, economic and media establishments, the 'Yes' campaign secured a decisive victory. Despite the NRC's focus on questions of sovereignty and identity, the dominant focus of the referendum coverage was on economics, and few ordinary voters heard the messages on sovereignty or politics. Many of those who voted 'Yes' in 1975 subsequently felt aggrieved. The refrain, 'I voted to join a Common Market' arose on doorsteps on countless occasions over the years, as disaffected citizens expressed their frustrations regarding the changes they believed had occurred in the UK's relations with the EU, thanks to repeated treaty reform. That voters, as opposed to parliament, had not voted to **join** anything at all was rather beside the point: many voters believed that the Community was essentially a trading arrangement and remained unaware of the inevitable loss of sovereignty that it entailed, even before the Community began to evolve into the EU with its common currency and wider policy aspirations. The fact that so many believed they had joined a common market was testament to the fact that most pro-Marketeers had failed adequately to make clear the nature of the EEC and its intended destination: political union. For some, this deception was intentional, as Heath made clear years later. Others, including Richard Moore, the pro-European Liberal official (and father of leading Eurosceptic journalist Charles Moore), believed such a course was destined to lead to problems as voters realised they had been misled.[2] The events of 2016 would prove him right.

The two-thirds majority in favour of staying in the Common Market in 1975 was resounding and, for those advocating membership, it was the end of the campaign: the referendum had resolved the question definitively. Or so they thought. In practice, those seeking to leave the Community would resume their struggle almost as soon as the referendum result was announced. There was a marked complacency among those favouring membership who believed their job was done. Opponents of membership simply gathered momentum as the Community (and later the EU) engaged in ever closer co-operation, as it continued to 'widen' and 'deepen'. These changes long went unnoticed in the UK, as in other member states where treaty reform was not subject to ratification by referendum, as the government typically blamed the EC for things that went wrong or were not politically welcome, while taking credit for successes, ensuring that there was rarely any chance of good press for the EC/U, even if the increasingly sceptical media had wished to provide it. When citizens eventually became aware of the changes they were not impressed. Remainers did little to advance their cause over the years as they did not realise that they would face a renewed challenge to membership, albeit only decades later.

Finally 'In' – but as an Awkward Partner, not a Key Player

Having initially refused to join the ECSC, and having stood aside from the proposals for subsequent Communities, when the UK finally joined the EC it found it difficult to make its mark as effectively as it had hoped. In 1967, Labour Foreign Secretary George Brown had urged German Chancellor Willy Brandt to help get the UK in, 'so that we can take a lead'. This somewhat hubristic idea that, despite joining late, playing no part in shaping the Community, nor yet creating the alliances necessary to achieve influence within it, the UK would nonetheless be able to lead was one that recurred throughout the decades as British politicians vacillated between seeking to take the lead and sitting on the sidelines bemoaning the direction 'Europe' was taking. Neither of these positions would ultimately prove fruitful, given that membership of the EU requires governments to be able to build up strong and enduring bilateral relations, in order to be seen as a loyal and reliable ally and in turn to know which other member states can be relied upon. Over the years, British politicians would rarely be willing to acknowledge this, even while pushing the single market and deepening political co-operation: hence the UK's reputation as an awkward partner, always sceptical about further integration and unable to punch above its weight developed.

Notes

1 Traditionally those supporting membership of the EEC were known as pro-Marketeers; those opposed were anti-Marketeers. The concept of 'Euroscepticism' arose rather later, notably around the time of the Maastricht Treaty, discussed in Chapter 3.
2 Richard Moore, as administrator of the European Liberal Democrat and Reform group in the European Parliament in discussion with the present author, c. 1995. His words have resonated with her ever since.

3 Winning and Losing
Money, power and the politics of treaty reform

The clear decision to stay in the Community did not stop British frustrations with European integration, and as the Community evolved into the European Union the UK became ever less comfortable. On assuming office in 1979, just four years after the referendum in which she had campaigned to stay in the Common Market on Wilson's terms, Margaret Thatcher vowed to 'get our money back', a reference to the contentious issue of the UK's contributions to the European budget, which Wilson's renegotiation had failed to resolve. Her approach won her few friends in the Community but did ensure a financial victory – a victory which would shape the British debate for decades, as no subsequent PM could risk making concessions on the budgetary contributions, as Tony Blair found to his cost in 2004. Despite Thatcher's success, the lack of an irrevocable solution would ensure that the UK's budgetary contributions would form a central part of the referendum thirty years later. In the medium term, however, it allowed the UK and the Community to move forward. Thatcher briefly donned a constructive, integrationist mantle, calling for reforms in the common or 'internal' market, as part of what became the Single European Act. Yet success had its price. For many European leaders, notably Commission President Jacques Delors, the market reforms entailed the corollaries of social policy and economic and monetary union. The reforms would see the Conservatives become ever more reluctant Europeans, while the Labour Party gradually saw the opportunities membership offered and adopted a more enthusiastic stance. In the long term, however, the pursuit of these goals would open up a gap between the UK and the rest of the Community that would eventually become a chasm, contributing in no small measure to the decision to leave the EU thirty years later.

In, but not Enthusiastic

Following the 'Yes' vote in 1975, the Labour Party appeared to become reconciled to Community membership and MPs finally took their places in the European Parliament (or Parliamentary Assembly, as it was still formally called), having previously boycotted it pending the outcome of the renegotiation and referendum.[1] Yet if the UK's place in Europe seemed assured, it was scarcely as an engaged or enthusiastic player – far from George Brown's vision of a UK 'leading' in Europe, the UK seemed determined to remain at the margins of the Community. Having secured the UK's place in the Community and a total of four election victories, Harold Wilson shocked the country by resigning as PM and Labour leader in 1976. He was replaced by his Foreign Secretary, James Callaghan, who had done so much to secure the renegotiation and make the Government's case for remaining in the Common Market. As Prime Minister, Callaghan proved a rather cautious European, unwilling to support moves towards the European Monetary System, a Franco-German initiative, led by fellow leaders French President Valéry Giscard d'Estaing and German Chancellor Helmut Schmidt, along with Commission President Roy Jenkins (one of Callaghan's former Cabinet colleagues), and intended as a staging post for the EMU agreed at the Hague Summit in 1969 and elaborated in the 1970 Werner Report.[2] This decision would be only the first time the UK sought to remain outside moves toward EMU. So successfully was the commitment sidelined that Norman Lamont, who made his maiden speech to the House of Commons in support of the European Communities Bill, later admitted he had been 'shocked' when he read the Werner Report (Lamont 2016). Such ignorance of the commitments that the UK had undertaken by accepting the agreement at The Hague is commonplace: the ambitions of the Community were clearly laid out, but few in the UK seemed to notice. Schmidt and Giscard pushed ahead and the Exchange Rate Mechanism (ERM) was set up in March 1979. Where Jenkins saw an opportunity to reinvigorate the European project through an initiative that he believed would have economic advantages and help further integration, his erstwhile British colleague did not. Callaghan secured the UK's first 'opt-out' – though at the time the phrase was not used and the expectation was that all states would move together in convoy, effectively ensuring that integration would move at the speed of the most reluctant state, often the UK. Callaghan's decision may well have been the correct one for the UK and its citizens, but for a new member state seeking to embed itself in the Community, it was scarcely likely to win friends elsewhere in Europe, far less to assist any leadership aspirations.

Nor was the UK quick off the mark to introduce the necessary arrangements for direct elections to the EP, which were due to be introduced in 1978. Differences between the Labour Party and the tiny Liberal parliamentary party (on whose votes Callaghan relied for a governing majority) ensured that the first direct elections were delayed until June 1979. Direct elections had been envisaged when the Treaty of Rome was signed as a way of adding a democratic element to the integration process, but they were not introduced owing to difficulties agreeing a common electoral system for the elections. By the mid-1970s the integration process seemed to have stalled, in part because of the economic problems arising from the Middle East crisis and associated oil price shock that afflicted the Community just as the UK was joining.

As the Community seemed to offer fewer tangible benefits to its citizens – the memory of war was fast receding and benefits of long-term peace were thus less apparent – so public support was declining. Jenkins, a passionate pro-European who had resigned from the Labour shadow cabinet in the early 1970s over the party's increasingly Eurosceptic policy in opposition, was the UK's first and only European Commission President and one of the most active incumbents in the role. He believed that introducing the long-anticipated European elections might help renew the legitimacy of the integration process and hence of the Commission itself. The reality proved somewhat disappointing, particularly in the UK where turnout in the EP elections, just a month after Margaret Thatcher's landmark victory swept the Conservatives back into office, was the lowest in the Community at just 32.3%. At the time the lack of interest from political parties and the media as well as the (potential) electorate could be put down to proximity to the general election – activists were exhausted and the key battle (Westminster) had been fought – and the fact that European elections were novel; people had no experience of them and needed time to become acquainted with democracy 'beyond the nation state'. Moreover, at the time, the EP remained a weak institution, enjoying only limited budgetary powers and the right be 'consulted' on legislation, as well as the power to kick out the European Commission but no commensurate right to affect the appointment of its successor. That turnout should have been low and interest limited in 1979 was not surprising – supporters of integration were sure that it would be a mere matter of time before citizens began to focus on the European level of politics, particularly as the Parliament began to acquire more powers. In practice, these hopes and expectations would come to naught; British citizens increasingly viewed the EU as undemocratic and the EP as a toothless and costly entity, despite the profound changes that would come about as a result of repeated treaty changes from the SEA onwards. At the time, EP elections were the least of the UK's worries – the matter of its financial contributions was far more pressing.

Too High a Price? 'I Want my Money Back'[3]

Almost as soon as she became PM in May 1979, Margaret Thatcher attended her first European Council meeting. It is customary for newcomers to be relatively quiet when they first attend such gatherings as they get to know fellow Heads of State or Government and learn the ropes of EU decision-making. However, Thatcher had a burning issue that she felt could not wait, namely British contributions to the Community budget. When the chairman of the meeting, French President Valéry Giscard d'Estaing, sought to wrap up the first day's proceedings, Thatcher insisted that she should get the issue of the UK's budgetary contributions onto the agenda that day. As she later put it ' ... at my very first European Council I had to say "no"' (Thatcher 1993, p. 64). This would be the first of many times Margaret Thatcher said 'no' to her European colleagues. Her style was one ill-suited to the niceties of European diplomacy, where side conversations and taking the opportunity to get to know other leaders in the margins of formal meetings provide a vital way to build up trust, create alliances and thereby secure one's interests in the EU. It was a lesson David Cameron would learn only too late in his engagement with EU negotiations; indeed the only UK prime minister who fully understood the importance of such informal and bilateral engagement was Tony Blair. However, Thatcher had been led to believe – rightly at that time – that she could impede the process of European decision-making for as long as she needed to and adopted a determined stance that would secure the budgetary settlement she desired as well as a reputation for awkwardness (Major 1999). However, she had made her case for reform of the Community budget, an issue which would take five years to resolve.

Thatcher was clear that the budgetary arrangements agreed by Edward Heath and 'renegotiated' by Harold Wilson ahead of the 1975 referendum served the UK ill. As she noted in her memoirs, 'In 1975 a Financial Mechanism to limit our contribution had been worked out in principle: but it had never been triggered, and never would be, unless the originally agreed conditions were changed. As a result, there was no solid agreement to which we could hold our Community partners' (Thatcher 1993, pp. 62–63). For Heath, the matter had been a price worth paying for the prize of membership; for Wilson, there had been enough of a deal to enable him to keep the UK in the Common Market; Thatcher could see no reason to accept an arrangement which she believed to be wholly unjust. In rather more florid language, she outlined the problem as she saw it during her 1979 Winston Churchill Memorial Lecture in Luxembourg: 'I must be absolutely clear about this. Britain cannot accept the present situation on the Budget. It is demonstrably unjust. Is it politically indefensible: I cannot play Sister Bountiful to the Community while my own electorate are being asked to forego improvements in the fields of health, education, welfare and the rest' (quoted in Thatcher 1993, p. 79). Thirty years on the electors would indeed vote for what some believed would return £350 million a week to the UK, perhaps to that very same National Health Service (NHS) to which Thatcher had indirectly referred.

The budgetary question highlighted a marked difference in approach to European integration between the UK and founding member states, particularly France, which took the Community's 'own resources' and associated budget as an article of faith. What for Thatcher was an injustice was for the French a key part of membership of the Community: monies that states transferred to the Community coffers should be considered the Community's 'own resources', not member state contributions. The Foreign and Commonwealth Office (1982, p. 186) was keen to assert that this was not, as some of the UK's detractors assumed, 'trying to undermine the common basis of Community financing by insisting on a *"juste retour"*, i.e. getting back from the budget exactly what the British taxpayers put in'. Perhaps not, yet one graphic and superficially compelling analogy during the 2016 referendum came from Lord Forsyth, asking people how they would feel if they gave him a £20 note and he only returned £10. In every other context membership of a club entails a fee from which benefits accrue, not payments offset by the same amount coming back as some in the UK seemed to desire. The FCO's analysis of 1982 accurately captured what one might assume to be the essence of the scheme: 'transfers [...] should be from the richer to the poorer' (FCO 1982, p. 186). In the first decade of British membership of the Community this logic would have meant money flowing *to* the UK, which was the 'sick man of Europe' at that time; by 2016 it had one of the best performing economies and was one of the richest member states, so larger net contributions according to its changed financial position might have been appropriate had the EU been a state where fiscal transfers were the norm. But the EU had not become a state and the regular wrangles about financial contributions persisted, even if the principles had been agreed.

At the Dublin Summit of November 1980 Thatcher had argued that 'the arrangement [must] last as long as the problem' (Thatcher 1993, p. 81); she finally achieved her aim at the Fontainebleau European Council of June 1984, fully five years after first raising the issue. The UK's contributions would be subject to a rebate of 66% of the difference between its VAT contributions and any receipts it got from the Community budget. A satisfactory long-term solution had been found but, while it was clearly both more valuable and more durable than the mechanism that Wilson had negotiated, it was not set in stone. At every negotiation of the multi-annual framework it would be up for reconsideration, creating a recurring headache for Thatcher's successors as Prime Minster, whether Labour or Conservative, and providing the Leave campaign with one of its strongest lines in the 2016 referendum, essentially, 'It's a lot of money, the rebate's not guaranteed and we'd rather spend the money on the NHS', as will be seen in Chapter 6.

Crossing the Rubicon – the Single European Act (1986)

The resolution of the budgetary question provided a welcome opportunity for the Community to move forward in two other areas, both of which the UK supported and both of which would ultimately cause a rise in hostility to integration: enlargement and deepening in the form of the SEA, with its associated '1992' project to complete the internal or single market. Temporarily, however, the UK now began to play a leading role in the Community, as for once the interests of the three largest members – France, Germany and the UK – converged to give impetus to further integration.

In line with the UK's long-standing preference for European co-operation on trade, as well as her own neoliberal economics, Thatcher was keen to make the Community more competitive at a time when it seemed to be slipping behind Japan, having long been behind the USA. It was a view shared by the Commission and by European businesses, so she was pushing at an open door. More surprisingly, given her subsequent Euroscepticism, she proclaimed herself to be a European 'idealist' who 'genuinely believed that once our budget contribution had been sorted out and we had in place a framework of financial order, Britain would be able to play a strong positive role in the Community' (Thatcher 1993, p. 536). Yet her approach was one that brought with it a foretaste of the attitudes of those Leavers who thirty years later sought to bring down the European edifice in order to create something better, or at least in a British likeness. Speaking to Tory members of the European Parliament (MEPs) ahead of the 1984 EP elections and shortly before the budget issue had been finally resolved, she claimed, 'I don't want to paper over the cracks. I want to get rid of the cracks. I want to rebuild the foundations [...] I want to solve [the current problems] so that we can set about building the Community of the future. A Community striving for freer trade, breaking down the barriers in Europe and the world to the free flow of goods, capital and services' (Speech on 8 March 1984, quoted in Thatcher 1993, p. 537).

Thatcher's trade agenda sought to build on three of the four freedoms outlined in the Treaty of Rome – goods, capital and services. It notably omitted the fourth – labour – which was necessary for free movement of services but entailed a challenge to borders and the right of states to choose who should enter. A logical corollary, then, to the trade agenda, but a problem for a leader committed to a Gaullist vision of a Europe of nation states and the importance of determining who should be permitted to enter one's state. While there was no suspension of free movement of labour, which at that time was unproblematic, she successfully secured an agreement that: 'Nothing in these provisions shall affect the right of member states to take such measures as they consider necessary for the purpose of controlling immigration from third countries, and to combat terrorism, crime, the traffic in drugs and illicit trading in works of art and antiques' (SEA quoted in Thatcher 1993, p. 555). Following the White Paper on 'Completing the Internal Market' penned by Thatcher's hand-picked European Commissioner Lord Cockfield and the federalist endeavours of new Commission President Jacques Delors, the member states moved swiftly to agree a treaty that set a deadline for completing the market and brought EPC into the treaty framework for the first time. Facilitated by the ECJ's landmark *Cassis de Dijon* ruling of 1979, the SEA introduced the idea of bringing down trade barriers between the member states through the principle of 'mutual recognition'.

Other aspects of the Act would eventually come to haunt the UK. Aware that Greece had already begun to impede the integration process, as indeed the UK had done so successfully for the previous five years, and with Spain and Portugal – less industrialised states unlikely to be enthusiastic about trade liberalisation – waiting in the wings, moves were afoot to introduce qualified majority voting (QMV) for decisions relating to the internal market. Thatcher was persuaded to accept change in order to secure the benefits of freer trade that she sought. It was to prove a turning point in the development of the Community – and in the UK's relationship with it. Thatcher (1993, p. 555) claimed, 'We were on course for the Single Market by 1992. **I had surrendered no important British interest**; I had had to place a reservation on just one aspect of social policy in the treaty' (emphasis added).

In reality, the SEA would prove to have dramatic ramifications thanks to the introduction of QMV, which saw a loss of national sovereignty.

The Act was ratified by Parliament with no reference to the general public – the idea of ratifying a treaty by referendum was never seriously countenanced. Some MPs, notably Bill (now Sir William) Cash, immediately recognised the dangers of the Treaty, the importance of which the PM sought to downplay in the House of Commons (Thatcher 1993, p. 556). Concerned about the possible diminution of parliamentary sovereignty, Cash argued:

> ... one is left with serious worries about the way in which it will operate in practice and about the apparently significant increase in the powers of the European Parliament which will accrue at the expense of this House. I appreciate that the Council of Ministers can have the final say, but that is not the real world.
>
> In reality, constant accretions of power exercised within the Council, subject to the co-operation procedure as it develops, are gradually whittling away the powers of this House in relation both to scrutiny and to the manner in which legislation is devised.
>
> (HC Deb 5 March 1986, Col. 384)

Sir Edward Du Cann, meanwhile, expressed his concern over the prospect of political union:

> It is a great step towards the creation of a European super-state and of a European political union. The outstanding thing, the regrettable thing, is that this Single European Act has never been discussed in either House of the British Parliament.
>
> I do not comment on whether the treaty is desirable or undesirable. I say only that any attempt to suggest that the Bill is a minor matter and exists merely in order to facilitate the workings of the Common Market would be a confidence trick.
>
> (HC Deb 26 June 1986, Col. 487–88)

The Heads of State and Government had explicitly granted more powers to the EP in the form of a right to amend legislation – the so-called 'co-operation procedure' – in recognition of the fact that in areas where QMV operated there would be a 'democratic deficit' arising from the fact that national parliaments would no longer be able effectively to hold their ministers to account. This shift of powers to the European level, where decisions are taken by representatives of national governments rather than national parliaments, contributing to a loss of both national sovereignty and parliamentary sovereignty, underpinned the emerging notion of the democratic deficit; the repeated response to this was to give the EP further powers each time the treaties were amended. Such moves would in practice do little to persuade British citizens or their MPs sitting in Westminster that the EU was now more democratic – an issue that would become all too evident in the 2016 referendum.

The SEA would have far-reaching ramifications but few appeared to share the concerns of Cash and the other early sceptics about the loss of sovereignty which the Act entailed, and it was certainly not the subject of widespread public debate, far less ratification by referendum. There was no public outcry and, while there was some concern among MPs, there was no wholesale parliamentary rebellion. The concerns were well-founded – the SEA removed the UK's veto in some policy areas, thereby reducing national sovereignty and reducing parliamentary control, a situation that would be a feature of subsequent treaty change. Certainly the Europhile *Financial Times* recognised the significance of the changes, claiming 'the Commission has rightly exploded the fallacy that Europe can somehow enjoy the benefits of a market of 320m. people without substantial concessions of national sovereignty ... ' (*FT* quoted in Cockfield 1994, p. 50). Thirty years on, other Eurosceptics would trace their concerns back to the SEA, seen as the Rubicon before the altogether more controversial Treaty on European Union (TEU or Maastricht Treaty), which would mark the start of deep Tory divisions that were still being played out at the time of the 2016 referendum.

Hindsight is a wonderful thing. Thirty years on this incursion into national sovereignty and the continuation of moves for ever-closer co-operation appear almost inevitable and entirely predictable. At the time they did not. Thatcher claimed to have read the SEA – indeed it is inconceivable that she would not have done so; she was a trained lawyer, so it is also unlikely that she would not have understood it. But she missed its true import, persuaded by civil servants of the importance of QMV to securing the prize of the internal market. Widening and deepening went together as in the 1970s, and both were endorsed by the UK at the time.

The implications of the SEA were not solely in the areas of sovereignty or democracy. Commission President Jacques Delors was a shrewd policy entrepreneur who sought to move beyond the functional spillover that might have arisen from the SEA, to 'cultivate' spillover in terms of both social policy and EMU. His calls for European-level social policy would have the twin effects of making the Labour

Party, which had become bitterly opposed to the Community in the early 1980s (going so far as to pledge to leave in its 1983 general election manifesto), more supportive of the Community while the Conservatives shifted in quite the opposite direction. EMU, however, was something that united many politicians across the political divide – Labour PM Callaghan had sought to keep the UK out of the ERM; his Tory successor was no more favourable to the ERM or to calls for full-blown EMU. Logical spillovers and long-standing commitments or not, neither social policy nor EMU enthused British Conservatives.

Indeed, the moves would inspire Margaret Thatcher's Bruges Speech of 1988. While in many ways a constructive contribution to the debate on the future of Europe, in which she explicitly reaffirmed a view that she had espoused at the time of the 1975 referendum: 'Britain does not dream of an alternative to the European Community, of some cosy, isolated existence on its fringes. Our destiny is in Europe, as part of the Community' (Thatcher 1988, p. 242), the speech became a lightning rod for Euroscepticism within the Conservative Party. Thatcher expressed the Gaullist view, completely at odds with the founding fathers and contemporary federalists such as Delors, that 'willing and active co-operation between independent sovereign states is the best way to build a successful European Community' (Thatcher 1988, p. 243). With a degree of foresight, she argued: 'If we cannot reform those Community policies which are patently wrong or ineffective and which are rightly causing public disquiet, then we shall not get the public's support for the Community's future development' (Thatcher 1988, p. 244); David Cameron would find this to be to true, to his cost, in 2016.

Among those policies that the UK would consistently deem to be wrong in principle and practice was economic and monetary union. Delors's attempts to press EMU resonated with some European leaders and at the Madrid European Council meeting in June 1989 the decision was finally taken to move ahead with EMU in three stages. Delors's proposals looked very similar to those that had been proposed by Werner nearly two decades earlier and were anathema to Thatcher. She did eventually agree to Britain participating in the early stages of EMU, on the condition that the UK would not be part of the final stage, namely the irrevocable union of European currencies. Despite the enthusiasm of Delors and the French it is possible that EMU would have stalled again: it was not popular in Germany and the Bundesbank was hostile. At the time Helmut Kohl was seen as a weak Chancellor and it is not clear he would have been able to get EMU through. However, a dramatic turn of events in autumn 1989 was to alter fundamentally the dynamics of integration.

The Collapse of Communism in Europe and German Unification

Thatcher's self-proclaimed vision for Europe included those in the East, who had long been on the other side of the Iron Curtain. The events of 1989 which marked the beginning of the end of Communism in Europe would provide her and other leaders with the opportunity to make good their interest in Central and Eastern Europe in the coming years. The reality proved rather more challenging than anticipated, and the associated reunification of Germany led to problems for the UK's European policy as, in the short term, British politicians struggled to come to terms with the new political realities and in the longer term as Germany began to play the more significant role in Europe that many of them feared.

While the reunification of Germany was a long-standing aspiration of the Federal Republic and its allies, by the 1970s it had seemed increasingly unlikely ever to occur. When it came, reunification was greeted with considerable anxiety in several states, including France and the Netherlands as well as the UK. (And this despite a quarter of a century of European integration, which might have been expected to have fostered mutual trust among the member states.) Convening a controversial meeting at Chequers, Thatcher believed it was necessary both to understand 'what a united Germany would be like' and 'to devise a framework for Europe's future taking account of German unification and the sweeping changes in the Soviet Union and Eastern Europe' (Powell 1990). The nature of the discussions and the fact that such a meeting was deemed necessary were indicative of a deep-seated mistrust that nearly two decades of Community membership had not removed.

In July 1990 the British Trade and Industry Secretary, Nicholas Ridley, caused a furore by giving an interview to Dominic Lawson of *The Spectator* in which he discussed monetary union: 'This is all a German racket designed to take over the whole of Europe. It has to be thwarted' (Ridley quoted by Lawson 1990, p. 8). Ridley was promptly forced to resign and the matter might have been of no more than passing interest had it not been for the fact that the views he articulated were not so far from those of the PM. As Lawson (1990, p. 9) noted, 'The point is, Mr Ridley's confidence in expressing his views on the German threat must owe a little something to the knowledge that they are not significantly different from those of the Prime Minister, who originally opposed German reunification, even though in public she is required not to be so indelicate as to draw comparisons between Herren Kohl and Hitler.' Moreover, Ridley's comments would foreshadow the Leave rhetoric a quarter of a century later, as he talked of the role of the President of the Bundesbank, Karl Otto Pöhl, and raised concerns about accountability and British reluctance to do what others exhort them to do: 'You can't change the British people for the better by saying, "Herr Pöhl says you can't do that." They'd say, "You know what you can do with your bloody Herr Pöhl."' (Ridley quoted by Lawson 1990, p. 9).

Meanwhile, Delors spotted his opportunity finally to secure EMU. Chancellor Kohl was determined to press ahead with unification regardless of the views of his EC partners but he was aware of the dangers of a German Europe. As John Major put it, 'As a student of German history, he never forgot his country's past, and his aim was to embed his nation securely in the Europe of the future' (Major 1999, p. 267). The best way to do so would be to bind Germany ever more tightly into Western Europe through membership of EMU, or so Delors persuaded Kohl. The UK thereby lost the support of the state previously assumed most likely to help it keep EMU off the table (Spence 1991). The UK position, at least as outlined in the Chequers Minute, was a little different, although the issue of binding Germany in was the same: 'We wanted Germany to be constrained within a security framework which had the best chance of avoiding a resurgent German militarism.' There was much talk of NATO and rather less of the Community – indicative of a view prevalent among many Conservatives and most Eurosceptics that it was NATO that had kept the peace in Europe – and some scepticism about Germany's commitment to integration:

> There were differing views over how genuine the Germans were in saying they wanted a more integrated Europe in parallel with unification. Was it just a tactic to reassure others? Or a genuine desire to subsume the latent nationalist drive of a united Germany into something broader? The latter was not wholly convincing, given that the structure of the EC tended to favour German dominance, particularly in the monetary area.
>
> (Powell 1990)

The questions of Europe and membership of the ERM would play their part in the departure of Thatcher and two of her senior ministers, Foreign Secretary Sir Geoffrey Howe and long-standing Chancellor Nigel Lawson. During the summer of 1989 she demoted Howe and then Lawson resigned, believing she listened to her advisor Alan

Walters rather more than to him over matters of monetary policy. Relations with Howe finally descended to such a point that he too resigned, giving a resignation speech that contributed to the PM herself losing office in November 1990. 'Europe' had claimed its first victims in British party politics; they would not be the last, and the legacy of Thatcher's defenestration by her own party would be seen in the divisions over membership of the EU for the next quarter of a century, starting almost as soon as her successor, John Major, who as Chancellor had persuaded her to join the European Monetary System, began his quest to take the UK to the 'heart of Europe'.

The Maastricht Watershed

The European question went to the heart of government, engulfing Major's premiership even more than it had done Thatcher's final days in office as he grappled with moves to establish a 'European Union', thanks to Delors's persistent commitment to further integration and the changed context of German unification, which jointly led to the Maastricht Treaty – one of the most controversial moves in the history of European integration, and one which would fundamentally damage British attitudes towards it. The citizens of Denmark rejected the Treaty; in the UK dissent over Maastricht was fomented rather closer to the heart of government. Whereas the SEA had been ratified with relatively little opposition from within the Tory ranks and certainly with no prospect of a referendum to ratify the revision to the founding treaties, the situation with Maastricht rocked the government of John Major.

Thatcher's successor was a pragmatic but constructive pro-European, not swayed by the federalist vision of Heath but nonetheless willing to engage with European colleagues. On taking office, he pledged to put Britain 'at the heart of Europe' and swiftly ensured that his party was more fully engaged within the mainstream centre-right of European politics by negotiating an arrangement whereby Conservative MEPs would sit with the Group of the European People's Party (EPP) as allied members. This allowed the Conservatives to benefit from being part of a larger grouping in the EP than had hitherto been the case, enabling them to secure key positions within the Parliament, including as Committee Chairs or vice-chairs and, crucially, meaning that the party leader could attend the eve-of-summit meetings with fellow centre-right party leaders. Since much preparatory work is done at such meetings and the opportunity to meet more informally and get to know colleagues is a vital part of doing business within the EU, this proved a shrewd move by Major; its unpicking by David Cameron 17 years later was a serious error of judgement to which we shall return. Nor did the access to the 'top table' entail any undue political compromise – their curious status as 'allied members' meant that the Tories could enjoy the benefits of being part of a large group in the EP without having to sign up to the (typically federalist) manifestos of the EPP at the five-yearly EP elections.

Major recognised that his country was not wholly committed to the direction in which leaders of some other European states wished to go. The collapse of Communism in Europe and, especially, the fall of the Berlin Wall and reunification of Germany had served as a catalyst for further deepening of integration. Plans for EMU were already underway in the framework of an IGC but it is not clear that Germany would have acquiesced to EMU had it not been for its dramatically altered status: a reunited country, no longer the two favoured by Mauriac and others, but a potential hegemon. As already noted, Chancellor Helmut Kohl recognised that this created anxiety in other member states and therefore undertook to bind Germany more closely into (Western) Europe by committing Germany to EMU. This political decision was intended to demonstrate a desire to create a 'European Germany' rather than a 'German Europe' in the words of Thomas Mann, a means, Kohl hoped, of averting German hegemony.

Alongside EMU, Kohl also wanted 'political union'. A second IGC was thus convened to deal with the new proposals, although it was far less thoroughly prepared than the IGC on EMU. The ensuing Maastricht Treaty created a pillar structure comprising a *communautaire* 'first' pillar covering the three original communities – the EEC (now renamed 'the European Community'), the ECSC and Euratom – and the newly established commitment to EMU, due by the end of the 1990s – three decades after the Hague Summit; a second, intergovernmental pillar covering security and defence; and a third pillar covering 'co-operation' in the areas of justice and home affairs (JHA). It also introduced the controversial concept of European citizenship, which conferred no responsibilities on the new European citizens but granted them certain rights, including voting in local and EP elections in whichever EU member state they were living. The Treaty also expanded the rights of free movement from those of workers ('labour' in the founding treaties) to 'people'. While citizens hoping to move to study, live or work in other EU states were still required either to be economically active or have sufficient resources to live on, it was a fundamental shift that altered the dynamics of free movement between member states, ultimately contributing to one of the most bitterly contested aspects of the 2016 referendum.

The initial proposals for what became the TEU went too far for Major. He managed to get the idea of a 'federal vocation', anathema to many in the UK, dropped in favour of a 'new stage in the process of creating an ever-closer union between the peoples of Europe, in which decisions are taken as closely as possible to the wish of the citizens' (*Agence Europe* 1991, p. 268), although in practice the subsidiarity clause was mostly forgotten or ignored in the UK. 'Ever-closer union' was already in the preamble to the Treaties and was seen by Major as preferable to more federalist language; for many Eurosceptics it implied the unpalatable idea that integration would inevitably undermine the nation state, even though the commitment related to people not states; it would later become the subject of David Cameron's renegotiation.

In order to proceed, each of the then 12 member states (Spain and Portugal having joined in 1986) had to agree and ratify the proposals. Traditionally the process of integration had been at the speed of the slowest, or the least integrationist, state and treaty reform required unanimity. The UK could thus have blocked the TEU. On this occasion, however, a precedent was set: recognising that it would be impossible to get the UK and Denmark (like the UK, always a reluctant member) to agree to certain aspects of the Treaty, notably EMU, it was agreed that they could opt out of those aspects they could not tolerate, permitting the treaty to go ahead without incurring a British (or Danish) veto. Thus the UK opted out of EMU and stayed out of European social policy, thanks to a protocol to the Treaty. On the face of it, this solution was a great success for the UK: it was not required to accept further deepening of integration in areas it did not support, but could play a full role in areas it believed to be beneficial.

The reality would prove far more challenging and would sow the seeds for the divisions in the Conservative Party that would play out in the referendum almost a quarter of a century later, as the detail of the Treaty became apparent – and unwelcome to many Conservatives including Margaret Thatcher. Major hailed the final Treaty as 'a success for the United Kingdom and the Community' (*Agence Europe* 1991, p. 270). Certainly, there was little for Major to celebrate. The Maastricht Treaty in many ways proved to be 'A Treaty too Far' as Michael Spicer (1992) called it at the time. Yet the immediate reaction to the opt-outs secured by Major and his Chancellor Norman Lamont and Foreign Secretary Douglas Hurd was very favourable within the Tory ranks in Cabinet and Parliament (Major 1999, p. 288). Meanwhile German Chancellor Kohl hailed the Treaty for quite the opposite reason: 'the way is paved for a further stage in the process of European unification,' which was now 'irreversible' (*Agence Europe* 1991, p. 271).

Two electoral processes ensured that ratifying the Treaty would prove remarkably difficult. On 9 April 1992 the Conservatives narrowly won the UK general election, which at one stage Labour had looked likely to win. With a majority of just 21 and with a raft of new, young, Eurosceptic MPs such as Bernard Jenkin elected among the new intake, Major would have enormous difficulty securing a parliamentary majority for the treaty. Then in June 1992, Denmark's constitutional requirement for a referendum to ratify the Treaty led to rejection by its citizens. This was the first time that a European treaty put to the people had been rejected. The outcome 'not only shocked the Danish government and parliament which realized that they were facing a serious communication problem with their electorate, but also caused a shock-wave throughout the whole of Europe' (Vanhoonacker 1994, pp. 4–5). Yet if there were shock waves across Europe, they were not enough to derail the Treaty. Rather, member state Foreign Ministers met on 4 June and agreed: 'The ratification process in Member States will continue on the basis of the existing text and in accordance with the agreed timetable before the end of the year.' The Conclusions of the European Council held in Edinburgh in December 1992 made certain changes and clarifications to the Treaty which, it was agreed, would be lodged with the United Nations – in other words, they would be valid under international law, not subject to the ECJ, which was itself a subject of mistrust in Denmark. The Danish voters were then asked to vote again on the Treaty in May 1993. On the second occasion they endorsed the Treaty, which came into force later that year once all member states had ratified it according to their own constitutional requirements.

As a one-off, and in the light of the complexity of the TEU and the fact that changes had been made after the Danish 'no', perhaps this might not have been a cause for concern. However, the treatment meted out to Denmark would not be the last time citizens seeking to reject élite-led treaty changes would be told to think again. The sense that élites were out of touch with their citizens was not resolved by reform of élite attitudes or behaviour, but by attempts to get citizens to change their minds – an odd approach to democracy and one that would be used against the EU in the 2016 referendum. (Indeed, so concerned was the present, pro-EU author about this tendency to ask voters to think again that she made a point of stressing in referendum debates that 'leave means leaving the EU', i.e. not some trial run before giving the establishment the answer they want to hear, nor an opportunity for a re-run. This was not a universally held view, as will be shown in Chapter 7.)

In the UK, John Major delayed ratification until after the Danes had voted again, thanks to an Early Day Motion seeking to defer ratification (see Baker at al. 1994, p. 39), and found Parliament hostile to the Treaty. There were 61 debates and 70 votes on the matter before it was finally accepted, as a result of Major turning it into a vote of confidence (Forster 2002, p. 99), causing Baker et al. (1994) to refer to a 'parliamentary siege of Maastricht'. Why was the Treaty so unwelcome? Apart from the content of the Treaty itself (which still included EMU which became even less popular in the wake of 'Black Wednesday' when sterling fell out of the ERM which it had finally joined in 1990, even if the UK had secured an opt-out), the increase in the number of sceptic MPs coupled with its very small majority created problems for the Government. These two aspects were compounded by the activities of Thatcher. Where she had read the SEA and agreed it, even if she might later have come to regret the loss of sovereignty it entailed, she also read the TEU and, most emphatically, did not agree with it. She proceeded to talk to backbenchers about her concerns, inviting them to drinks parties during which she 'would go through the Maastricht Treaty and say what was wrong. The backbenchers then said they couldn't support it' (Forsyth 2016). Many erstwhile Thatcherites would later become the most passionate advocates of leaving the EU. Indeed, the European fault lines in the Conservative Party can to some extent be traced back to the fraught attempts to ratify Maastricht, where the lines were between Thatcherites and Majorites (Baker et al. 1993; Clarke 2016, pp. 30, 316). As Major himself noted, when the TEU was being proposed, ' ... the direction of European policy was a pathological source of division within the Conservative Party. The wounds from Margaret Thatcher's departure were still fresh and showed little sign of healing. Her most devoted supporters had convinced themselves that her policy of resisting European integration was the principal cause of her fall. They were sure to oppose any change in that direction' (Major 1999, p. 265). Lest there was any doubt about Thatcher's drift from moderate pro-Europeanism to outright hostility, she sent a letter to Bill Cash in 1993, requesting 'that the letter be published in the event that anyone tried to suggest that she was in favour of closer European integration' (William Cash 2016, p. 25). The letter stated: 'I understand that it is being suggested in some quarters that I would have agreed to the Maastricht Treaty. May I make it clear that I would *not* have done so. In my view, it is contrary to British interests and damaging to our parliamentary democracy.' (Quoted by Bill Cash's son William Cash 2016, p. 25.)

While Major did finally secure parliamentary ratification of Maastricht, his party would remain deeply divided over the EU and a new issue had been put on the agenda – the idea of another European referendum. Having eschewed the idea of ratifying the SEA by referendum, in November 1991 Margaret Thatcher called in the House of Commons for a referendum on the single currency. The Cabinet was divided, with some figures on both sides of the European debate opposed to a referendum 'on constitutional grounds' (Major 1999, p. 275). The Maastricht rebels similarly sought to amend the Bill 'to require the Government to hold a national referendum on the treaty in the belief that public opinion had become hostile to Maastricht's implications' (Baker et al. 1994, p. 38). While such calls came to naught in the early 1990s, they marked the start of a growing movement for a referendum, whether on membership of the euro, as the common currency came to be known, or Treaty reform or, as those most passionately opposed to the EU really wanted, the existential question of whether to be in or out. They also led to the emergence of new anti-EU movements that would challenge the Conservatives electorally and contribute to a hardening of Conservative rhetoric against European integration: UKIP, founded by left-wing sceptic Alan Sked; and the short-lived Referendum Party of Sir James Goldsmith. While calls for a referendum remained low-key in the 1990s, the demands for the public to have their say were taken up by the leaders of all three main parties, who committed themselves to holding a referendum before taking the UK into the euro. Such promises would become a constant refrain but they were to remain unfulfilled for two decades, causing growing frustration in the country, not least among grassroots Conservatives.

Notes

1 Members of the European Parliament were drawn from national parliaments until the first direct elections were held in 1979.
2 While the Six agreed on the principle of EMU in 1969 they differed over whether economic convergence or monetary union should come first. Luxembourg PM Pierre Werner was therefore asked to produce a report on the matter. He recommended a compromise approach in three phases, which would provide a blueprint for the creation of the euro a quarter of a century later.
3 To misquote Margaret Thatcher, as so many commentators do. She did not actually demand **her** money back but the UK's.

4 Leaving the People Behind

Aside from facilitating the reunification of Germany and serving as a catalyst for deepening integration through the creation of the Maastricht Treaty, the collapse of Communism in Europe had a profound impact on the geographical limits of the EU, as it led to unprecedented demands to enlarge the newly created European Union. For once, this provided an opportunity for the UK to play a constructive role. British politicians agreed with their European partners that enlarging the EU to the Central and Eastern European states that were emerging as fledgling democracies and seeking membership of a whole range of Western institutions was a natural and necessary consequence of the end of the Cold War. For over a decade, enlargement and the prospect of enlargement dominated the European agenda in terms both of negotiations with aspirant neighbouring states and of securing the institutional reforms necessary to allow the EU to function efficiently and effectively after a near doubling of its membership. Moreover, despite the UK's stated preference for enlargement, there was little support for the constant treaty revisions which it necessitated. These interrelated changes converged to create unanticipated problems for the UK as the EU budget and the UK's hard-fought rebate came up for review, and free movement of EU citizens from the new member states led to unexpectedly high numbers of newcomers seeking to live and work in the UK. The associated institutional reforms contributed to further frustration among citizens, who were repeatedly given the prospect of a referendum only to see it vanish like a mirage. As under Thatcher with the SEA, so changes promoted by the UK under Tony Blair would turn into problems contributing to the case put forward by those seeking to leave the EU.

Enlargement – Widening and Deepening, and the Tensions between the Two

The Maastricht Treaty marked the high point of European integration in many ways. Highly ambitious and far-reaching, it fulfilled the ambitions of federalists and others, like Delors, while retaining national constraints in policy areas that went to the heart of national sovereignty, such as foreign and defence policy, and allowing opt-outs in areas where the UK and Denmark, in particular, sought them. The Treaty reflected the concerns of Cold War Europe, not the dramatically altered nature of the continent after 1989, which saw several newly-emerged democracies seeking membership, bringing different historical experiences and geopolitical concerns from those of the existing member states and, to a lesser extent, from each other. As the EU sought to adapt to take on board the would-be new members, a series of treaty changes would come about – some helping to prepare the Union for enlargement, some ostensibly envisaged as helping bring the EU closer to its citizens. While the former ambition, actively promoted by the UK, was achieved, repeated attempts to engage citizens had the perverse effect of creating ever more distance from them. And as the years passed and successive governments continually failed to deliver on their promise of a referendum, the European question became ever more politically charged in the UK.

For the UK, the prospect of expansion has generally been seen as desirable for precisely the reasons that France was cautious about allowing enlargement in the first place: a wider Community/Union was likely to be a weaker one, they believed. Germany, by contrast, was always of the opinion that widening and deepening could run in tandem, rather than being mutually exclusive. For decades it seemed that the EU could keep expanding in terms of members and powers, as states sought to join a successful project and the Union amended its rules to mitigate the effects of enlargement, usually also deepening at the same time. Thus, Thatcher was persuaded to accept QMV in the Single European Act precisely because of the pending accession of Spain and Portugal. Clearly enlargement was seen by some as a way to thwart further European integration, although Thatcher had for once been trying to stop newcomers impeding deepening, which in this instance coincided with British objectives. Major also favoured enlargement, even famously suggesting he could envisage Europe expanding 'at least as far as the Urals'. (How he proposed to persuade Russia of the benefits of dividing that country was never explained.)

Labour PM Tony Blair, who took office in May 1997, favoured expansion – fast. It was assumed by some that he wished to impede

European integration, though in practice he seemed to be genuinely of the view that what was good for the UK was good for other states as well, including those CEE states that had so recently come out of Communism. Here there were similarities with the German position: Germany felt that having benefited from European integration for 40 years, it could not but open the EU to states that had suffered during the Cold War. The 'big bang' enlargement of 2004 that saw ten new states join, including eight from Central and Eastern Europe (known as the A8), along with Malta and Cyprus, would have significant consequences for the EU itself, involving institutional reform, budgets, immigration and free movement; as well as more divergent interests, as was the case with every enlargement, but now magnified by the sheer scale of the proposed expansion.

In terms of the EU budget or Multiannual Financial Framework (MFF), a paradoxical situation arose whereby the UK's budgetary rebate, as negotiated originally by Margaret Thatcher and subject to review at the time of every periodic MFF, was due to rise dramatically as a result of the accession of a set of much less well-off states. The reason for this was straightforward: the rebate was still calculated on the basis of the gap between the UK's gross contributions to the EU and any monies received back such as CAP payments and monies from Structural Funds. With the accession of the much poorer CEE states, the UK would receive a smaller amount of revenue from the Union, net contributions would therefore rise and, hence, the size of the rebate would also rise in proportion to net contributions. While an increased rebate was wholly in line with the deal negotiated in 1984, the Labour government accepted that it was not justified in the context of eastward enlargement; indeed it was felt to be morally reprehensible to accept this increased rebate, which would inevitably have entailed these new poorer countries themselves contributing towards the British rebate. However, Blair's decision was met with opprobrium at home and it was clear that any future reduction in the rebate would remain politically suicidal in the UK. The print media, in particular, devoted many column inches to deriding Blair for surrendering part of the rebate – criticism that he failed to rebut by making the straightforward case that a rebate on the back of the poorer states would be manifestly unjust.

The Labour Government also accepted that citizens of the A8 countries should be able to exercise free movement from the moment of accession on 1 May 2004. This was despite the fact that the EU had agreed a seven-year transitional period during which existing member states could impose restrictions on the free movement of people from the new CEE member states. The UK was the only member state apart from Ireland and Sweden to open its doors to unlimited free movement immediately. At the time the UK was enjoying an economic boom and high levels of employment, hence the Government believed that it would benefit from an expanded labour force. However, the UK was wholly unprepared for the sheer scale of inward migration that would occur. The Government had been told to expect 13,000 net newcomers a year. The reality was over 400,000 (Watt and Wintour 2015). The higher than expected numbers, alongside a failure to plan (or even to prepare the ground) for significant numbers of new EU citizens arriving in the UK, would gradually create a context for increased opposition to the EU little more than a decade later, when immigration, often conflated with free movement, formed a key part of the heated Brexit debate.

Traditionally seen as too controversial to constitute a key part of mainstream party political activity, immigration began to take centre stage from the 2005 general election. On that occasion, the Conservatives, led by Eurosceptic former Home Secretary Michael Howard, ran a poster campaign stating: 'It's not racist to impose limits on immigration.' While this may have been correct just a year after EU enlargement, the other mainstream political parties did not engage with this issue, and it was not politically salient at the time. By the 2010 election, UKIP, the party whose *raison d'être* was about leaving the EU, also began to raise the issue of immigration. By this stage the full implications of A8 accession and its impact on the UK in terms of newcomers from those countries, particularly Poland and Lithuania, were beginning to feed into the public debate. This was most graphically highlighted during the campaign in an embarrassing encounter between Labour PM Gordon Brown and a Labour voter, Gillian Duffy, who had raised concerns about immigration. As he walked away from his interlocutor, Brown expressed frustration that he had been made to talk to a 'bigoted woman'. Unfortunately for him, his words were caught on microphone. In the furore that ensued what was perhaps ignored was the fact that Duffy was accurately reflecting a shift in thinking among ordinary, often Labour-leaning, voters. Over the years many had become concerned about the changes in their communities, as witnessed in the different goods, especially groceries, on sale in local high streets in some parts of the country. That Mr Brown was so surprised by her attitude in many ways reflected how far removed he – and indeed many Westminster politicians – were from the everyday concerns of citizens. It is perhaps not surprising that, six years on, Duffy would be voting to leave the EU while Brown was actively advocating staying in.

Preparing to Enlarge – the EU needs to Reform Itself Too

With the prospect of several newly emerging democracies with fragile transitional economies seeking membership, the EU finally established a set of membership criteria in 1993, more than two decades after the first enlargement. The so-called 'Copenhagen criteria' stipulated that would-be member states had to meet certain standards of democracy and human rights, as well has having a functioning market economy and the ability to integrate their legislation into the *acquis*. Unless they could meet such standards, aspirant states would not be permitted to join. The aim, as always with enlargement, was to ensure that a larger EU would not be a weaker one. In addition, the EU itself needed to undertake reforms to ensure that the institutional arrangements would be fit for purpose once the Union enlarged. The process would prove fraught and time-consuming. From the mid-1990s until 2009, the EU found itself constantly preparing for reform, revising the treaties and then ratifying (or failing to ratify) those treaty reforms.

The Treaty of Amsterdam

Almost soon as Tony Blair had been elected Prime Minister in 1997, the 1996/97 IGC culminated with the Treaty of Amsterdam. Long planned and referred to as IGC 1996, the final stages of the IGC were deferred by fellow EU leaders in the expectation that the increasingly awkward Major Government would be replaced by Labour, which had now become the more pro-EU of the two main UK parties. As they hoped, Blair immediately provided a more constructive approach than Major had in his final days in office and the Treaty was agreed without undue difficulty. The treaty amended policy around immigration and made some institutional reforms, but otherwise was quite insignificant. Blair signed the UK up to European social policy, unpicking the social protocol to which Major had devoted so much time as a way of keeping social policy out of the Maastricht Treaty. While marking an improvement in UK-EU relations, the Amsterdam Treaty failed in its main objective of preparing the EU for eastward enlargement. The EU might have been rhetorically committed to enlargement, but member states seemed reluctant to bring about the changes required to allow newcomers to join. This to some extent mirrored the rather slow progress the CEE states were making towards meeting the Copenhagen criteria. Further treaty reform would thus be required if the prospective enlargement was not to harm the Union's ability to function.

The Treaty of Nice

The 15 member states (Austria, Finland and Sweden having joined in 1995) made relatively swift progress on reform after Amsterdam. More substantive institutional reform was enshrined in the Treaty of Nice, agreed in 2000, which finally paved the way for enlargement to Central and Eastern Europe, giving rise to various reforms that would fit the EU institutions for a near-doubling of membership from 15 to 25 and later 28. Larger states lost their second Commissioner but more significant reforms collapsed when Irish voters initially rejected the Treaty, persuaded by the rhetoric of the 'No' campaign, which claimed that Ireland would lose power, influence and money. The grievance was less the treaty *per se* and more the reality of enlargement, which would mean countries like Ireland, which had been among the poorest member states and hence were significant net beneficiaries of EU membership, would see reduced financial rewards and enjoy relatively less influence as a result of the 'club' expanding.

Various changes were made to the Treaty, including the significant decision not to cut the size of the College of Commissioners to fewer than the number of member states as originally envisaged – Ireland would keep 'its' Commissioner – an odd point, given that, once appointed, Commissioners are strictly forbidden from taking instructions from their home country, but one that is symbolically important nevertheless. When asked to vote again in 2002, the Irish duly accepted the modified treaty. Again, it was clear there was a gulf between élites and peoples. Member state leaders were by then acutely aware of this problem, so much so that they had already announced at Nice that there was a 'need to improve and monitor the democratic legitimacy and transparency of the Union and its institutions, in order to bring them closer to the citizens of the Member States'. The Swedish and Belgian Presidencies of the Union were asked to look at these issues and in December 2001 the Laeken Declaration asserted that: 'The Union needs to become more democratic, more transparent and more efficient. It also has to resolve [...]: how to bring citizens, and primarily the young, closer to the European design and the European institutions, how to organise politics and the European political area in an enlarged Union.' A key problem within the EU had been identified, but the proposed solution would bring with it many more problems than it solved and would ultimately exacerbate the UK's European problems and mistrust of the EU generally.

The Convention on the Future of Europe

In contrast to previous patterns of treaty reform, where an IGC had undertaken the preliminary work before the national leaders finally sat around the negotiating table, it was decided to widen the process of consultation. Thus was born the Convention on the Future of Europe (also known as the European Convention). It was presided over by former President of France, Valéry Giscard d'Estaing, with a senior British diplomat, Sir John (now Lord) Kerr, himself a veteran of the Maastricht Treaty negotiations, serving as its Secretary. Each of the 15 member states and 13 candidate countries was entitled to send two representatives of their national parliaments and one government representative. Fifteen MEPs also participated and two Commission representatives, plus two Vice-Presidents. This was already a large deliberative body, but it was augmented by substitute members who could attend and speak (though not vote) even if the full member was present. In addition there was a 'forum' to allow ordinary citizens to participate, although in practice it was attended by representatives of Brussels-based organisations, ensuring that while there was an element of engagement by civil society there was little grassroots involvement, leading the long-standing Danish Eurosceptic MEP Jens-Peter Bonde to suggest it was 'Brussels talking to Brussels'.

To oversee the work of the Convention, a 12-member Praesidium was created, among whose ranks sat a British representative: the Labour MP for Edgbaston, Gisela Stuart, who would become a leading player in the Leave campaign in 2016, one of the few from among Labour ranks. At the time seen as pro-European – Blair even referred to her in his memoirs as 'very New Labour' (Blair 2010, p. 320) – Stuart argued for an enhanced role for national parliaments in EU decision-making, notably calling for a 'red card' to allow them to block legislation (Stuart 2002). She would subsequently claim (Stuart 2016) that it was her experiences with the Convention that turned her against the EU, believing that it had lost any sense of subsidiarity (taking decisions as close as possible to the people) – a key aspect, along with participation and solidarity, of the Catholic social teaching which had underpinned the thinking of the EU's founding fathers, and which John Major had been keen to enshrine in the Maastricht Treaty in preference to any formal references to federalism. At the time Stuart had argued:

> We need to review and consolidate what we have, to succeed with our reforms, succeed in enlarging the Union and in linking our national systems more closely to the European level. There is a

perceived crisis of legitimacy and citizens evidently feel disillusioned with and disconnected from the institutions. There is a lack of trust, and we have to acknowledge this.

(Stuart 2002, pp. 10–11)

This was, of course, precisely the reason the Convention had been convened in the first place. The irony was that the mechanism intended to reduce the gulf between political élites and the citizens would in practice lead to a much wider chasm.

The Convention, which met from 14 February 2002 until July 2003, took up its work with enthusiasm – it was given four specific institutional questions to address, each intended to respond to the concerns raised about the lack of democracy and transparency. However, led by Giscard, the members of the Convention opted instead to draft a full-blown constitution for the EU. It was far from the mere 'tidying-up exercise' that the UK Government representative Peter (now Lord) Hain claimed. It did 'tidy up' certain issues, but it also made some profound changes to Union decision-making, entailing further loss of national sovereignty through the expansion of QMV. The proposals provided, *inter alia*, for an elected Commission President, a fixed-term President of the European Council (something Stuart [2002, p. 11] had been advocating) and a European Foreign Minister. There was much scope for these leading figures to engage in 'turf wars' had the proposed treaty ever come into being. In short, there was much to worry British voters and politicians concerned about sovereignty. However, the Treaty establishing a Constitution for Europe was rejected by the citizens of two founding member states, France and the Netherlands, although it was a decision of the UK that acted as a catalyst for this dramatic turn of events.

A Referendum Pledge

Breaking with convention, Tony Blair proposed to hold a referendum to ratify the Constitutional Treaty. He believed he had little choice. Ever since the Maastricht Treaty debacle there had been growing calls for the UK to hold a referendum on the European Union. Having rejected the use of referendums while PM, Thatcher had led the calls for a referendum on the Maastricht Treaty and then become a key figure in the Eurosceptic Bruges Group (named in honour of her 1988 speech there). Alongside the emerging Eurosceptic wing of the Conservative Party, for which Thatcher became a focal point, two other groupings emerged to press for a referendum. The first was the aptly named Referendum Party, created and funded by Sir James Goldsmith. Goldsmith put a huge amount of his own money into fielding 547 candidates in the 1997 general election (House of Commons Information Office 1999), and while no Referendum Party candidate was elected, the movement had a considerable effect on the political landscape, contributing to the Conservatives losing seats to Labour – as Goldsmith anticipated (William Cash 2016, p. 26).

The growing Euroscepticism in the print media had contributed to Major's woes in 1997 but had also fostered an enduring Euroscepticism against which the pro-European political mainstream – Tory, Labour or Liberal Democrat – was unable to gain traction, as both Blair and Cameron would discover. Four titles had been bought by Australian businessman and Eurosceptic Rupert Murdoch, who was assumed to exert a degree of influence over his editors. Stuart Higgins and Trevor Kavanagh, respectively editor and political editor of *The Sun*, told the Prime Minister's office that they were trying to stop Murdoch requiring their paper to back Labour in the 1997 general election but that 'it would be Europe that weighed most heavily on the newspaper's decision' (Seldon 1998, p. 711). In the event, *The Sun* did back Labour – a decision that arguably affected Blair's subsequent decision not to hold a referendum on joining the euro in 1997. Another Murdoch title, *The Times*, was ambivalent about which party to support but demonstrated just how far the European question had permeated political, electoral and media discourse. Rather than endorse a single political party, *The Times* recommended 'its readers should back the most Eurosceptic candidate in their constituency' (Seldon 1998, p. 710). The Conservative response was enlightening in terms of the 2016 referendum. They 'highlight[-ed] the inconsistency of the position in supporting [veteran right-wing Eurosceptic] Alan Clark and at the same time the left-wing Labour MP Jeremy Corbyn' (Seldon 1998, p. 710). In the end, the European question did not determine the 1997 general election. The Labour landslide owed more to wider dissatisfaction after 18 years of Tory rule. However, the incoming Labour Government was notably more pro-EU than Major's administration by the time the latter left office.

For the first time, 'Europe' was beginning to affect the electoral dynamics of the UK, notably causing problems in Conservative seats. Such changes would be compounded by the emergence of the UK Independence Party from 1993. Initially very much a fringe organisation, UKIP gradually gathered momentum, making incursions into Tory-held seats. With the introduction of proportional representation for EP elections in 1999, UKIP secured parliamentary representation, winning three seats in the EP. At each successive EP election its support rose, as it took seats and votes mostly (but not exclusively) from the Conservatives, whose response was to adopt an increasingly sceptical stance. UKIP's electoral success had an added bonus: MEPs enjoy various financial allowances for administrative purposes, which helped the emergent party to build its position, creating a virtuous circle (for UKIP at least) of increased funding which helped it to secure more MEPs, thereby further helping the party's cash flow and infrastructure as it became more electorally successful. A party that had been created to oppose the EU was in practice enriched and empowered by the very body it sought to destroy. Against this new electoral challenge Tory MPs, parliamentary candidates and the grassroots membership began to strengthen their Eurosceptic rhetoric, though to little obvious effect. In the 2009 EP elections, UKIP came second to the Tories, securing 13 seats in the EP and fuelling further anxiety and rhetorical Euroscepticism within Conservative ranks. The depth of Tory Euroscepticism in constituency associations is clear from the fact that candidates for the 2010 general election were reputedly all asked the same question in seat selections: 'If you could repeal one piece of legislation, what would it be?' The expected – and for many grassroots members the only acceptable – answer was 'The 1972 European Communities Act'. The die was cast for a new Parliament in which there would be a large number of new MPs thanks to the parliamentary expenses scandal the previous year, which had led many MPs to decide not to stand again in 2010. Many of the newcomers were committed to leaving the EU. Yet UKIP was not simply gaining support in Tory former heartlands. Just as the Referendum Party had helped Labour in 1997, so 'Nigel Farage's UKIP helped Cameron to a majority victory in 2015, by taking traditional working-class Labour votes in key Midlands and northern marginals' (William Cash 2016, p. 26). This fact was perhaps overlooked during the 2016 referendum by the Remain campaign, which had assumed that the Labour heartlands would follow the official line of the party leadership. In practice many erstwhile Labour supporters had already drifted towards Euroscepticism and it was those traditional Labour heartlands that would contribute to the unexpected Leave victory. Labour Party leader Jeremy Corbyn's apparent reluctance to campaign passionately in the referendum could have been vindicated, however; with hindsight, his attitudes towards the EU appeared more in line with those of traditional Labour voters than were those of many in his Parliamentary party.

But all this is to jump ahead. When New Labour took office it was as a positive pro-European party, seeking to put the UK at the heart of Europe, as Major had tried and failed to do. However, *en route* to electoral success in 1997, Tony Blair had courted Rupert Murdoch and had tempered his own pro-Europeanism to some extent. Against the background of the emergence of the Referendum Party, the 1997 Labour manifesto promised a referendum before any decision to take the UK into the euro (Seldon 2005, p. 317). Blair's sweeping victory in the general election meant that a referendum on joining the euro could have been held alongside the referendums on Scottish and Welsh devolution in September 1997, during New Labour's 'honeymoon period'. Yet no referendum was held and gradually the UK's chances of joining began to appear ever slimmer, given the actions of the Treasury under Gordon Brown, who, like David Cameron who had been advisor to the Chancellor Norman Lamont at the time of Black Wednesday, had been marked by the UK's earlier forray into the precursor to EMU. Blair's own position on the euro was more akin to Major's than might be expected. While Blair appeared the more passionate advocate of the euro, both men felt that they could only take the UK into the euro if the conditions were right – and they never were. Thus, as the years went by the promise of a referendum slipped away. And as former Foreign Secretary Robin Cook noted, the events surrounding the war in Iraq (which began in 2003) ensured that the public no longer trusted the Government, stating that: 'the bigger obstacle to a successful referendum is that the credibility of the government has been a casualty of the war' (Cook 2003, p. 169).

At the time of the Constitutional Treaty, Blair again offered a referendum, albeit reluctantly: 'With deep misgivings, I accepted we had to promise a referendum on it. We wouldn't get the Constitution through the House of Lords without it, and even the Commons vote would have been in doubt' (Blair 2010, p. 501). That the Commons vote to ratify the Treaty should have been in any doubt shows just how divisive the European question was in both main parties: Blair had a large Commons majority, unlike Major or Cameron, yet still could not be sure of securing a vote. The referendum pledge gave Blair a further problem – the media:

> … it [the prospect of the referendum] reminded me how far I had to go to persuade British opinion of the merits of being in the mainstream of Europe. As ever, the difficulty was that the Eurosceptics were organised and had savage media backing; those in favour of a constructive attitude were disorganised and had the usual progressive media 'backing', i.e. spending more time criticising their own side than rebutting the propaganda of the other.
>
> (Blair 2010, p. 501)

The media landscape described by Blair would only be magnified a decade on when the UK did finally hold a referendum on the EU. Pro-Europeans had been silent for too long, while the sceptics had turned up the volume and the media had presented a consistently Eurosceptic message for decades.

Blair was released from his referendum pledge by the voters of France and the Netherlands. Neither country needed to hold a referendum to ratify the Treaty any more than the UK did. However, French President Jacques Chirac believed that 'If Britain promised a referendum, it put enormous pressure on France to do the same' (Blair 2010, p. 501). Several other countries followed suit, with dramatic consequences for the Union. Having only narrowly endorsed the Maastricht Treaty by referendum in 1992, on 29 May 2005 the French rejected the Constitutional Treaty. On 1 June, Dutch citizens, voting in their first ever national referendum, rejected the Treaty even more resoundingly. Blair's reaction on hearing the French result was one of relief: 'I knew at once I was off the hook' (Blair 2010, p. 531). Foreign Secretary Jack Straw's reaction was unalloyed: 'Great news' (Blair 2010, p. 531). Surely the Treaty was dead. No-one could ask the French to vote again, as they had asked of the Irish and the Danes. Straw immediately called for a 'period of reflection', although the Luxembourg PM, Jean-Claude Juncker, announced that his country would hold its planned referendum in which Luxembourgers duly voted to ratify the Constitutional Treaty. Thereafter it appeared moribund.

The reflection period lasted for two years until 2007, when German Chancellor Angela Merkel, holding the rotating EU presidency, pressed ahead with the reform process. The European Council meeting in June that year agreed to launch a new IGC, placing institutional reform back on the European agenda. Blair was indeed 'off the hook', having already left office, but the UK did have to participate in the IGC, and it would have to ratify the resulting treaty.

The Treaty of Lisbon

By the time the replacement for the Constitutional Treaty was negotiated in 2007, Blair had been replaced as PM by Gordon Brown. Seen as rather a reluctant European during his time as Chancellor, Brown was in fact committed to the EU but he insisted on various 'red lines' before accepting what became known as the Lisbon Treaty. The new Treaty differed from its rejected predecessor by virtue of being a revision to the existing treaties (as had been the SEA, Maastricht and other reforms), rather than a free-standing document. Thus, Brown took the view that it was not necessary to offer a referendum. His decision was wholly in line with those taken on European matters (be it to join the Community or to ratify treaty reforms) by every incumbent Conservative Prime Minister, even if Thatcher would hold a different view once she had left office. Yet Brown's attitude was at variance with Blair's commitment over the Constitutional Treaty and decades of increasingly virulent calls for a referendum on the EU. Moreover, former European Convention President Valéry Giscard d'Estaing went out of his way to stress that the Lisbon Treaty was essentially just the Constitution by another name (Giscard d'Estaing 2007); and that it was a federal document. As if to reinforce this claim, Spain took the decision that no referendum was needed to ratify the Lisbon Treaty, because its citizens had already voted on the Constitutional Treaty.

Brown's decision was not welcomed by either of the main opposition parties in the UK. The Conservatives argued that there should be a referendum on the Lisbon Treaty as Blair had promised over its aborted predecessor. Party leader David Cameron stated that his party would hold a referendum if it came into office before the Treaty had come into effect. The Liberal Democrats took a slightly different stance, with party leader Nick Clegg claiming that there should be a referendum not just on the Treaty but on the broader question of whether or not the UK should be part of the EU at all. The strongly pro-European former MEP had been won over by the logic that no-one under 55 years of age (or thereabouts) had had a say in 1975, and so they should be given that opportunity. While clearly a case could be made for holding referendums on constitutional matters, the idea of repeating the experience at intervals was novel to say the least. The idea was not welcomed by many senior Liberal Democrats, who remembered the experience of 1975 and did not think it desirable to repeat it. Nonetheless, Clegg, perhaps inadvertently, had tapped into a proposal whose time had (almost) come. The EU had become such a divisive issue in British politics that a referendum might be the only way to resolve concerns. Eurosceptics had long advocated such a move; some pro-Europeans managed to persuade themselves that this would be the way to resolve the issue, safe in the 'knowledge' that, of course, British citizens would opt to remain in the European 'club'.

Seeds of our Own Sowing

The UK's determination to see the EU enlarge, compounded by two crucial decisions – to give up part of the UK's hard-won budgetary rebate and to allow immediate access to the UK labour market[1] –

helped create the conditions in which calls to leave the EU would thrive, even though that initial decision to allow free movement from the moment of enlargement was taken in a very different economic climate from that facing Gordon Brown in 2010 or the Remain campaign in 2016 after years of austerity, or at least a narrative of austerity. The Lisbon Treaty was a missed opportunity finally to bring Europe closer to its citizens; something that was sorely needed if it was to secure legitimacy in the eyes of British voters. Indirectly, Tony Blair's decisions over the budgetary rebate and free movement (like Thatcher's decisions on QMV and John Major's acquiescence over EU citizenship and the associated rights of free movement of people *qua* citizens and not just workers) also contributed to the decision to leave the EU, as gradually UK citizens began to feel that the EU and indeed their own country had changed beyond all recognition. These views were in part accurate; in part based on perceptions (in some cases misperceptions); and in part attributable to the lies and half-truths that infected the referendum campaign on both sides. Free movement of people would become deeply entwined with the wider, and politically toxic, issue of immigration more generally; a fact that both the official Leave campaign and its unofficial allies – Leave.EU – would deploy very astutely in their campaigns to take the UK out of the EU. By the time New Labour left office, the Conservative Party was deeply Eurosceptic and UKIP was making inroads into its support, paving the way for a perfect Eurosceptic storm that ultimately led to the 2016 referendum.

Note

1 While Maastricht had changed to requirements to permit free movement of 'persons' rather more generally than 'labour' as outlined in the founding Treaty of Rome, it was workers that the Labour government sought to attract ahead of the 2004 enlargement when the UK economy was booming.

5 Seeking to Reconcile Conservatives and Coalition

The surprise outcome of the May 2010 general election – a coalition between the staunchly pro-EU Liberal Democrats and the increasingly Eurosceptic Conservatives – looked set to put the European question centre stage in British politics for the first time in decades. Could two such different parties co-operate on so contentious an issue? In practice, the formal Coalition Agreement, and the fact that Prime Minister David Cameron was keen that questions about the EU should not dominate his time in office, ensured that the differences between the parties were not much in evidence, at least at ministerial level. Two clear commitments – to what became the EU Act 2011, enshrining in law a provision that there should be a referendum whenever substantive powers were to be shifted to the EU level, essentially at the time of treaty reform, and for a Balance of Competences review to assess whether the EU was interfering in too many policy areas – successfully kept the truce between the parties for much of their time in office. By contrast, there was marked dissent within the Conservative Party as many, particularly Eurosceptic backbenchers, took the opportunity to challenge the Prime Minister on EU affairs. They were frustrated with a leader who had failed to secure clear electoral success and had thus delivered a coalition with Europhile Liberal Democrats – who had both taken jobs in government that might otherwise have been theirs and (or so Cameron's detractors felt) had watered down Cameron's resolve in a whole range of policy areas including 'Europe' (Smith 2015). Since the Government had a parliamentary majority of nearly 80, these backbenchers could rebel on European matters, secure in the knowledge that they were acting in line with their party's grassroots and were in any case unlikely to bring the government down, ironically precisely because of the presence of Liberal Democrats in government.

As the rebels became ever more vocal in their opposition to the EU, Cameron sought to placate them by standing up to other EU leaders in

Brussels, first trying to veto proposals for a new treaty to tackle the eurozone crisis, then over the European budget, and finally in opposing the nomination of the centre-right Luxembourg federalist Jean-Claude Juncker as Commission President. However, none of Cameron's actions reduced the temperature among those in his own party demanding a referendum on the UK's membership of the EU – a referendum many felt had been delayed for too long. Having whipped his MPs to reject proposals for a referendum in 2011, in January 2013 Cameron finally accepted the idea. In his now famous Bloomberg Speech, a rather pro-EU speech in many ways which nonetheless garnered support from those hostile to the EU within the Conservatives, Cameron pledged to hold an 'in/out' referendum by the end of 2017 if the Conservatives were re-elected in May 2015. This promise, along with the associated themes of reform (of the EU) and renegotiation (of the UK's relationship with the EU), proved successful in the short term, as his party held together on Europe during both the 2014 European Parliament and 2015 general elections with the line 'Reform, renegotiation, referendum: UKIP can't; Labour and the Lib Dems won't; only the Conservatives will give you a referendum'. Nonetheless, UKIP came first in the 2014 EP elections with almost 30% of the popular vote.

Growing Conservative Euroscepticism

The divisions that had emerged during the ratification of the Maastricht Treaty persisted through the prolonged period in opposition as the Conservatives elected a series of Eurosceptic leaders committed to keeping the UK out of the euro. Three successive leaders were all keen to burnish their Eurosceptic credentials. William Hague, who had come to prominence aged 16 when he spoke at the Conservative Party conference, was perhaps too young when he became leader of the Conservative Party, and certainly the one general election he fought as leader saw the Conservatives trounced. The campaign was memorable for its anti-euro focus, marked by a countdown of 'X number of days to save the pound', in recognition of the Conservatives' argument that Labour would take the country into the euro despite the lack of evidence for such claims. As Foreign Secretary under David Cameron, Hague, while remaining Eurosceptic, would ultimately argue that the UK was better inside the EU than leaving it. His two successors as Conservative Party leader, Iain Duncan Smith and Michael Howard, would not only invoke Eurosceptic rhetoric as leaders of the Opposition but also campaigned to leave the EU in 2016, with Duncan Smith in particular playing a leading role in the Leave campaign.

By the time Michael Howard stood down as leader in 2005, the EU had become a bitterly divisive issue within the Conservative Party. In order to secure a place in the second ballot among party members David Cameron made only one policy pledge: to withdraw his party from the group of the centre-right European People's Party in the European Parliament. To most ordinary voters this would have meant little then or later. Few would have heard of the EPP and it played no direct role in British political life. However, Cameron was focused on securing votes from Eurosceptic Conservative MPs in order to get sufficient support to go through to the ballot of Party members. In practice Cameron's short-term tactic was to have significant long-term ramifications for the Conservative Party and for the UK's position in the EU. Membership of one of the largest groups in the European Parliament confers considerable benefits, notably influence within the EP and the other EU institutions. In particular, party leaders meet with their opposite numbers from sister parties ahead of European Council meetings; it is at such side meetings that the crucial preparatory work is done, and where leaders get to know each other informally and build up the sort of relationships necessary to find friends and allies with whom to take decisions at European level. Taking the Conservatives out of the EPP would create major difficulties for David Cameron as he sought to negotiate with other leaders, leaving the UK less able to influence decision-making than it would otherwise have been.

Initially, it seemed that there were no natural allies for the Eurosceptic Conservatives. Following his election, Cameron despatched Shadow Foreign Secretary William Hague to travel around Europe to look for potential partners in a new EP grouping. Hague's view was that there were none, and the matter appeared to have been dropped. Three years later, in early 2009, Cameron announced to a stunned EPP that he would be withdrawing his MEPs from the EPP group after the 2009 EP elections. The announcement met with hostility in the EPP and caused considerable short-term damage to relations with the Christlich-Demokratische Union Deutschlands (CDU) and its leader Angela Merkel (not to mention Klaus Welle, the Secretary-General of the EPP who would go on to be Secretary-General of the EP). However, the pragmatic German Chancellor recognised that on many issues – not least of which was the need for austerity in the wake of the global financial and eurozone crises – she had more in common with Cameron than with successive leaders of France (with whom Germany had been allied by default ever since the 1963 Elysée Treaty) and a close working relationship with Cameron developed. Nonetheless, the Conservatives' absence from the EPP caused considerable problems for

Cameron as time and again he found the dictum 'if you are not at the table, you are on the menu' to be vindicated. At times this seemed to play to his advantage at home, certainly within his own parliamentary party – for example, when he sought to veto the Fiscal Compact Treaty or block the appointment of Jean-Claude Juncker as European Commission President. Yet in the longer term the Conservatives' lack of reliable allies at the European level would prove a problem. Over time Cameron learned the importance of bilateral relations, but there was a tendency to assume that the relationship with Merkel would be sufficient to enable him to secure his preferred outcomes. It was not, and never could be, since Merkel, like Cameron, was heading a coalition Government and was subject to the will of her electors and to media scrutiny – facts that successive UK politicians seemed to neglect in their approaches to EU decision-making.

Into Coalition

The result of the 2010 general election came as a shock to the pundits: the first hung Parliament in a generation; a coalition Government for the first time since the end of the Second World War; and Liberals in government for the first time in nearly a century.[1] While the results might have been unexpected by most, and unwelcome for many, some scenario planning had been done behind the scenes. The negotiations that produced the 2010 Coalition Agreement within just five days of the general election were miraculously short compared with similar endeavours in other European states. Both parties believed that the global and eurozone crises, notably the problems facing Greece, meant it was essential to come to an agreement as swiftly as possible 'in the national interest' to ensure that markets remained stable. This mantra would persist through the coalition period and the austerity narrative would contribute to some of the dissatisfaction voters (especially on the left) felt towards the EU by the time of the referendum. The impact of the coalition's policies would further highlight disparities between various communities, with those feeling 'left behind' more prone to oppose EU membership.

'Europe' was one policy field where the two parties looked set to face the greatest disagreement. The Liberal Democrats had long been seen as the most pro-European party. Even when they sought to downplay their pro-EU credentials, as frequently occurred in EP elections, they were portrayed as zealous Europhiles. Yet their leader Nick Clegg, although committed to British membership of the EU, was not uncritical, having long advocated its reform. As an MEP, he had argued the

EU should not interfere in the 'nooks and crannies' of member states. Nonetheless, the Liberal Democrats and their Liberal antecedents were historically most out of tune with their electors: the most pro-EU party did not have the most Europhile electors.[2] Thus during election campaigns it was not uncommon for voters to say on the doorstep that they would be voting for the Liberal Democrats locally and UKIP in the EP elections on the same day. That Liberal Democrats, to a greater extent than the other main UK parties, tended to focus on local issues perhaps made this split-voting a rational approach on the part of electors – an approach, however, that made it harder for the Remain campaign when the time came for a national referendum. Indeed, the general apathy and complacency about the EU that characterised the behaviour of all the supposedly pro-EU parties for decades would come back to haunt them in 2016, when the decision to focus on local and state elections before giving serious attention to campaigning on the referendum saw them outflanked by a Leave campaign that had just one target: 23 June, viewing the local elections as a mere staging post to the main event.

By 2010, the Conservatives were deeply divided over the EU but were broadly sceptical. Moreover, after nearly two decades of calls for – and promises of – a referendum on the EU, whether on membership of the euro, treaty ratification or the fundamental question of membership, there were calls for Cameron to make good his promise to hold a referendum on the Lisbon Treaty when he took office. This would have made no sense given that the Treaty had already come into effect in December 2009, as Foreign Secretary William Hague (formerly somewhat of a 'poster boy' for Tory Eurosceptics), made clear – to the frustration of harder-line sceptics. Pragmatism was to the fore within the Conservative arm of the new coalition, and Europe was not a priority as the Government sought to deal with the financial crisis and austerity politics, a situation that was not welcome among disaffected backbenchers. The European dividing lines were clear and they were within the Conservative Party itself, rather than between the two coalition partners.

Two factors ensured that 'Europe' would be a problem for Cameron. Firstly, the balance of the new intake of MPs was more strongly Eurosceptic than in the previous parliament, rather as the new intake challenging Major had been in 1992. The difference was that now the newly elected MPs were reflecting the views of their constituency associations. With a few notable exceptions, they had been willing to say they wanted to repeal the 1972 European Communities Act – some may have said it simply in order to secure selection but many of the new intake were committed to the cause of leaving the EU. Yet a Eurosceptic cohort of MPs would not necessarily have led to Europe dominating public, or even political, discourse. Their underlying concerns were given oxygen and space to develop by the fact that Cameron had not won the 2010 election outright – hence the need for a coalition, which caused considerable frustration among Tory backbenchers. For some it was a matter of principle: Bill Cash, for example, opposed coalition with the Liberal Democrats precisely because of their views on the EU, and wrote to tell Cameron so, arguing that other arrangements might be acceptable but a coalition was not because 'it would guarantee that they would not be able to pursue a Conservative policy over the EU' (Cash 2014). His warning went unheeded.

Many, though not all, of those who opposed the coalition were – like Cash – also vehemently Eurosceptic, which provided a perfect storm for a PM keen to sideline Europe as an issue. As one long-standing pro-EU MP put it, there were 'A large minority of irreconcilables, about 20 to 30, who were very anti-EU.' Yet, as the MP pointed out off-the-record in 2014, eighteen months before the referendum:

> 'The Eurosceptics are divided. There are the "old guard" represented by John Redwood, Bill Cash and Bernard Jenkin who feel that their time has come and they will get what they want in 2015 with a majority government. Second, a new generation including [Douglas] Carswell see them as dinosaurs refighting old battles. They want to bring the Conservatives back together [with UKIP], see for example Jacob Rees-Mogg in *The Mail*.'
> (Off-the-record interview with senior MP, 8 September 2014)

Douglas Carswell was to defect to UKIP in 2014, as was fellow Tory MP Mark Reckless, both causing by-elections which the Tories lost before the 2015 general election. The vast majority of 'irreconcilables' were deeply committed Conservatives, however – they were not about to leave their party, but they were absolutely determined that their views on the EU should prevail. That they were ultimately able to hold sway was in part a result of Cameron's inability to manage his own party, which was the very reason the referendum was called in the first place.

Cameron's problems were in part a direct consequence of the coalition and his failure to get his colleagues onside. Whereas the Liberal Democrats had a complex but ultimately democratic process for agreeing to the terms of the Coalition Agreement, including votes by all parliamentarians and a special members' conference, Conservatives were offered no such opportunity to express their views. As many backbenchers on both sides of the European divide complained, there was not even an opportunity for a show of hands at the 1922 Committee (the body that brings together backbench Tory MPs). Not only had Cameron failed to win the election and formed a coalition with the pro-EU Liberal Democrats, these new partners had taken ministerial jobs that would otherwise have been theirs. Cameron's apparent failure to listen or consult made handling the EU issue within his own party even harder. Moreover, over the course of the coalition, 'the Conservative leadership was driven by events' (according to the senior MP interviewed by the author in September 2014), lacking a strategic vision on European matters. Initially the Liberal Democrats also paid little attention to EU matters; 'their' minister in the Foreign and Commonwealth Office, Jeremy Browne, took his role to be 'anything but Europe' as several interviewees put it. The dynamics of coalition thus offered considerable scope for Tory Eurosceptics to set the agenda on an issue that mattered more to them than to almost anyone else at that time. Pro-Europeans repeatedly complained that Cameron giving way to the sceptics was like feeding red meat to the dogs: the more he gave, the more they wanted. Ultimately, as the rest of this volume shows, the 'old guard' would triumph. Yet at the outset of the coalition the European issue seemed to be settled remarkably easily.

The Coalition Agreement

The Coalition Agreement set out the policies to which the two parties would be committed during their time in government. Its position on the EU was measured, including a commitment to the UK playing 'a leading role in an enlarged European Union' as so many governments had aspired to do previously, but also stipulating that 'no further powers should be transferred to Brussels without a referendum. This approach strikes the right balance between constructive engagement with the EU to deal with the issues that affect all of us, and protecting our national sovereignty' (HM Government 2010, p. 19). Liberal Democrats might not have chosen to refer to sovereignty had they been governing alone, but the Agreement was sufficiently constructive to be acceptable to them, while not immediately causing concerns for Tory Eurosceptics. Moreover, it had the merit of offering the prospect of a referendum without any likelihood that it would have to be delivered during the course of the Parliament (2010–15), ensuring that any existential questions regarding membership could be deferred for at least five years. After all, no enlargement (beyond Croatia as the 28th member state) was foreseen in the near future, so no major enlargement-related reforms were likely and no further treaty changes were otherwise envisaged, as the EU was seeking to focus on embedding the institutional arrangements enshrined in the Lisbon Treaty after more than two decades of reform.

The Coalition Agreement made two specific pledges that reflected the concerns of the partners regarding sovereignty and the powers of the EU: firstly, to introduce legislation to amend the 1972 European Communities Act so that any future transfer of sovereignty to the EU would be subject to a referendum, the so-called 'referendum lock'; and, secondly, to 'examine the balance of the EU's existing competences', which led to the Review of the Balance of Competences – a two-year project over 2012–14, resulting in the publication of a series of reports.[3] The 'referendum lock' spoke to both Conservative frustration at the fact that repeated treaty change ever since the SEA had ceded sovereignty to the EU without reference to the citizens and to the Liberal Democrat view that the UK should have another vote on whether or not to remain in the EU, albeit at the time of treaty reform, not at some random date. Liberal Democrats could thus argue that the time for any in/out referendum would be at the time of some far-off treaty reform, safe in the knowledge that this was not about to happen. The Review of the Balance of Competences arose from the Conservative view that the EU had acquired too many powers over the years; it was not something with which their coalition partners necessary agreed, but they were willing to accept the proposal. Three more commitments also spoke to traditional British concerns and/or ambitions: to remain outside the euro; to 'strongly defend the UK's national interests in the forthcoming EU budget negotiations'; and to 'support the further enlargement of the EU'. A further commitment coming from the coalition manifesto was to 'examine the case for a United Kingdom Sovereignty Bill to make it clear that ultimate authority remains with Parliament', but no progress was made on this pledge during the course of the coalition Government.

The Coalition Agreement made one fundamental constitutional change that would shift the legislative-executive relationship in the UK and affect the dynamics of the coalition on all matters, including EU affairs: namely to introduce legislation for fixed-term parliaments. Traditionally, one of the powers enjoyed by British PMs was the right to trigger a general election at the time of their choosing, allowing them to go to the country at the time they believed would give them maximum electoral advantage; it also acted as a brake on unruly backbenchers – bringing down a government and precipitating an election in which the governing party is divided is a recipe for electoral damage, so MPs taking the government whip were normally reluctant to inflict too many parliamentary defeats on that government. Thus, Major had secured the successful passage of the Maastricht Treaty by making the decision one of 'confidence' in his Government, once his parliamentary majority had been virtually eroded. The Fixed-term Parliaments Act 2011 sought to ensure that in normal circumstances the Parliament would run for a full five-year term. Liberal Democrats were particularly keen to secure this reform, as they believed it would prevent the Conservatives trying to cut and run from the coalition at a time to suit their own electoral interests. In practice the change, coupled with the comfortable Commons majority enjoyed by the coalition, meant that backbench Conservative MPs felt emboldened to rebel, safe in the knowledge that they were extremely unlikely to jeopardise the Government's majority, unlike the Major years when a slim majority had been undermined by the Maastricht rebels. Paradoxically, a tool intended to stabilise a government following the election of a hung parliament provided the context for internal party disputes which would jeopardise Tory party unity and ultimately pave the way for the momentous pledge to hold an in/out referendum.

Towards a Referendum

The European Union Act 2011 enshrined proposals for a 'referendum lock', stipulating that any subsequent transfers of competence to the EU were to be subject to a referendum. No longer would governments be able to cede powers without the explicit endorsement of citizens. While the Act did not go as far as the Coalition Agreement in that it failed to amend the 1972 European Communities Act (a source of concern for Eurosceptics) it did provide a check on the apparent ratcheting upward of European integration. Liberal Democrats were unhappy with the draft legislation and there was a general sense that Jeremy Browne had not been sufficiently attentive to his party's position while in the Foreign Office, hence eleventh-hour changes were demanded by the then Secretary of State for Energy and Climate Change, Chris Huhne (source: off-the-record interviews). Thereafter, anxious not to be outflanked, the party became more focused on European matters for the rest of the Parliament. Tory Eurosceptics, meanwhile, did not feel that the Act went far enough, a view shared by the viscerally anti-EU *Daily Express*, owned by Richard Desmond.

The *Express* thus ran a petition calling for an EU referendum. This reflected in part the pervasive nature of Euroscepticism in the print media, though the *Express* was especially notable for the vitriol with which it treated the themes of both EU membership and immigration, becoming the only newspaper to back UKIP in the 2015 general election.

Future defectors to UKIP Mark Reckless and Douglas Carswell were vocal supporters of the petition. Reckless called for 'as many people as possible' to sign, saying, 'I am extremely supportive of the wonderful campaign by the *Daily Express* which has helped push the debate onto the national stage'. Carswell said, 'The Government has said they want more direct democracy and I hope they welcome the *Daily Express*'s efforts to give us a chance to debate whether there should be a referendum on the EU' (*Daily Express* 2011). The *Express*'s petition was straightforward: 'We call on the Government to arrange for an orderly withdrawal of the United Kingdom from the EU by means of an enabling referendum. We want parliament to debate this.' The coalition Government had introduced a provision that petitions reaching more than 100,000 signatures could be considered for debate in the House of Commons. Thus, the newly convened Backbench Business Committee of the House of Commons scheduled a debate on holding a referendum.

By the time the matter came up for debate on 24 October 2011, the question had been further complicated. Three options, rather than the more conventional binary choice seen in most referendums, were proposed, giving Government and Opposition leaders alike an excuse to reject it. The motion, in the name of Conservative MP David Nuttall, read:

> That this House calls upon the Government to introduce a Bill in the next session of Parliament to provide for the holding of a national referendum on whether the United Kingdom should
>
> a   remain a member of the European Union on the current terms;
> b   leave the European Union; or
> c   re-negotiate the terms of its membership in order to create a new relationship based on trade and co-operation.
>
> (HC Deb 24 October 2011, Col. 46)

The leaders of the three main parties – Cameron, Clegg and Labour Party leader Ed Miliband – were united in their opposition to the proposed referendum and made their views on the matter exceedingly clear: each imposed a three-line whip on their MPs to vote against the motion. Given that the majority of MPs were in favour of remaining in the EU (the Labour Party had by 2011 adopted a solidly pro-EU stance like the Liberal Democrats, while many Tories would undoubtedly have supported the PM in rejecting a referendum), a free vote would have had the advantage of allowing Eurosceptics to express their opinions by voting in accordance with their deeply held views while not running any serious risk of securing a majority for the referendum. However, the imposition of a three-line whip ensured that the EU would be a running sore, at least in the Conservative Party. In the event 81 Tory rebels defied the whip and voted for a referendum. The vast majority were Eurosceptics (including Adam Holloway who resigned as a parliamentary private secretary in order to rebel), but their number did include some pro-EU MPs such as Mark Field, who believed it was time to resolve the vexed EU question and that an early referendum would provide the best way to secure a vote to stay in the EU. Many of those who rebelled were the usual irreconcilables, such as Cash, Jenkin and Redwood. Several MPs, including some who would subsequently play leading roles in the Leave campaign, voted with the Government rather than jeopardise their ministerial positions. Two notable Labour rebels who voted for the motion were Jeremy Corbyn and John McDonnell, at that time far from positions of influence in their party (HC Deb 24 October 2011, Division No. 372). The vote failed but the nature of opinion in the Conservative Party had been laid bare – almost every Tory speaker in the lengthy debate prefaced their remarks with 'I'm a Eurosceptic', regardless of which side of the referendum issue they finally came down on and whether or not they obeyed the whips. The depth of that sentiment would make it hard for Remainers to gain traction when the referendum finally came, as so many of those campaigning to remain were among the self-proclaimed Eurosceptics.

Shortly after the failed rebellion the UK found itself on the verge of an unanticipated EU treaty change which, if agreed by the member states, would have triggered the 'referendum lock' under the EU Act 2011. As already noted, the coalition had taken office in the wake of the global financial crisis and at the height of a eurozone crisis that threatened to bring down the common currency and possibly even the EU – at least according to Herman van Rompuy, then President of the European Council. While this scenario might have gladdened the hearts of hard Eurosceptics, Chancellor of the Exchequer George Osborne recognised that the UK had an interest in ensuring that the eurozone should not collapse, given the knock-on effects this would have for the UK economy. The logical solution was closer integration for the eurozone countries, leading to fiscal, and possibly political, union. The UK did not wish to be swept along by such changes, but nor could it sit entirely on the sidelines. Moves were afoot for a new treaty to tackle the eurozone crisis, with the normal round of pre-summit meetings – including a dinner for the party leaders and heads of state and government of the EPP family to which, having withdrawn the Tories from the EPP, Cameron was not invited. By the time of the summit, held in Brussels in December 2011, Cameron had a plan. However, he had neglected one of the first rules of EU decision-making – the need to have allies and to know they will support you. This requires careful preparation, usually in the form of bilateral meetings with potentially like-minded countries.

Cameron failed to build such alliances or to alert his counterparts to his proposals in advance. When, in the middle of the night, he finally produced his wish list – for a protocol allowing the UK to opt out of proposed changes in financial markets regulation – he won little support. Leaving the room, he claimed he had vetoed the treaty, much to the delight of Conservative Eurosceptics, who greeted the move enthusiastically on his return to Westminster. In practice the treaty did go ahead but without the UK or the Czech Republic; in a sense, therefore, Cameron had not vetoed it, but had merely avoided the UK becoming party to it. The Fiscal Compact as agreed was an international treaty, not an EU treaty, and thus not binding on the UK; a significant victory for a PM who perhaps did not wish to trigger the referendum lock of the EU Act 2011. Nonetheless the episode was a failure of diplomacy by Cameron, which caused a rift with his Liberal Democrat Deputy, Nick Clegg, who initially said he had been kept abreast of the negotiations and supported the PM, only to appear on the BBC's Andrew Marr show two days later to say how furious he was about proceedings. Nor did Cameron's apparent petulance in leaving the room endear him to his European counterparts. That the summit was ill-prepared in part reflected a shift in the manning of the UK's Permanent Representation (UKREP, essentially the UK's Embassy to the EU) from the FCO to Treasury officials, bringing in people with little experience of the niceties of diplomacy. In part it reflected a change in the arrangements for European Council meetings – previously the PM would attend with the Foreign Secretary or another minister; for the first time it was only the PM in the room, leaving him more exposed than he would otherwise have been. There were many lessons to be learned if the UK wished to exert influence within the EU.

The Bloomberg Speech – Changing the EU-UK Relationship

Refusing to sign up to the Fiscal Compact gave Cameron temporary respite, but his backbenchers continued their noisy opposition and eventually he changed his mind. In January 2013, at the London headquarters of the US news agency Bloomberg, he made a long-awaited speech outlining his own views on the UK's relationship with the EU. In many ways this was a rather pro-European oration which apparently had the approval of his Deputy, Nick Clegg. Although Clegg later expressed incredulity at Cameron's offer of a referendum (Clegg 2016, p. 206), the speech gave cheer to those in the PM's own party who sought to leave the EU. While paying fulsome tribute to the founding fathers and their ideals, Cameron listed a series of problems with the EU, called for powers to 'flow back to the member states', and asserted 'we need fundamental, far-reaching change'. Cameron stated that a Conservative Government would reform the EU, renegotiate its terms of membership and then hold a referendum on remaining in the EU by the end of 2017. The date was purportedly chosen to give the maximum time to negotiate reforms between various national elections, most significantly the UK general election in May 2015 and French and German elections in April/May 2017 and Autumn 2017 respectively.

The mood in the Conservative Party changed – and so did the Cameron's attitude to introducing legislation on holding a referendum. Thus when James Wharton came first in the ballot for Private Member's Bills (PMBs) in 2013 and announced his bill would be for a referendum on membership of the EU, he received active encouragement from the Party leadership, in marked contrast to the backbench debate just 18 months earlier. However, PMBs are rarely successful without government support, or time in the legislative calendar, and if the Conservative leadership's position on a referendum had changed, that of their coalition partners had not. Thus, Wharton's bill was not granted Government time and, while it made its way through the House of Commons, it was blocked in the House of Lords, as pro-EU peers from all parties sought ways to prevent the passage of a bill for which they could see no popular mandate. When they voted to stop the committee stage of the bill, it was effectively dead. The Conservative reaction was furious, with Wharton claiming: 'Labour and the Lib Dems have conspired in the House of Lords to kill this important piece of legislation, doing the will of their political masters in the Commons' (*Evening Standard* 2014). The prospect of a referendum was essentially on hold until such time as the Conservatives could secure a majority.[4]

Repatriating Powers

Apart from being determined to give the people a say over the future of the UK's relations with the EU, the Conservatives hoped to 'repatriate powers' from the EU, which they believed was overbearing and interfering. In order to assess which powers might appropriately be repatriated, the idea of evaluating the powers the EU already had was introduced into the Coalition Agreement. An objective analysis of the powers held at national and EU levels could be seen as a necessary precursor to arguing for repatriation of powers and reforms as a way of making the EU work better for the UK. In practice, the Balance of Competences review generated a vast amount of work for civil servants and ministers. It resulted in an extensive compendium of facts about the powers, which were deemed by the ministers overseeing the review to be broadly about right. 32 different reports were produced including on the thorny issue of the EU budget and the previously welcome theme of EU enlargement, alongside matters with clear and pervasive EU dimensions such as justice and home affairs or environmental policy, on the one hand, and on the other those, such as health policy, where the EU dimension was less immediately obvious. It was decided in advance that the reports would not contain conclusions, nor would there be any overarching review of the reports on which policy-makers could draw. Rather it was left to each political party to make use of the findings in whichever way it saw fit. This clearly made sense in light of the marked disparity in the views of the coalition partners, but it ensured that the reports gained little traction, being virtually ignored by policymakers, commentators and the general public. Certainly it seems they were not used in a meaningful way in any party's 2015 manifesto, nor in the 2015/16 renegotiation or the 2016 referendum. The Balance of Competences review was thus something of a missed opportunity for pro-Europeans to make their case, and was disparaged by sceptics.

The EU Budget and the MFF – Finishing the Job Thatcher Started

The Coalition Agreement pledged, 'We will strongly defend the UK's national interests in the forthcoming EU budget negotiations and agree that the EU budget should only focus on those areas where the EU can add value' (HM Government 2010, p. 19). The question of the UK's contribution to the EU had never entirely vanished. Annual wrangles of the sort encountered by Thatcher had largely been eradicated by the introduction in the late 1980s of multiannual financial deals. Yet, as Blair had found to his cost, these arrangements could prove even more difficult. His decision to hand back part of the UK's rebate following the 'big bang' enlargement of 2004 remained a source of criticism in the UK, and no British politician could do other than pledge to hold the EU budget down while hanging onto the British rebate. The Government's ability to deliver on the budget pledge was in some ways more assured than its prospects of delivering other commitments made in the Coalition Agreement. Cameron could indeed threaten to block a budgetary deal that was blatantly against UK interests, as unanimous voting meant that the UK had a veto. However the driving force behind success in securing a cut (in real terms) in the EU budget for the period 2014–2020 came not from steely determination in the ranks of the coalition Government, nor from the Conservative leadership, but from a parliamentary vote in October 2012. Labour MPs, along with 53 Tory rebels, joined forces to inflict the coalition's most serious defeat. The PM had pledged to veto a bad deal but believed that it would be difficult to negotiate anything less than an inflation-linked rise in the budget. The rebels, led by Mark Reckless, argued that the PM's hand would be strengthened by receiving a parliamentary mandate to go further and reduce the EU budget in real terms; something that was previously unheard of. Reckless argued: 'If you think the EU has too much money, its budget is too large and it needs to be cut, then vote for the amendment' (quoted in BBC News 2012). As he put it to the BBC, 'the UK was "fed up" of giving more money to the EU every year and MPs had made clear a budget cut was the "only thing" they would accept. "What this is about is our constituents' money," he said. "Parliament has spoken very clearly that unless there is a deal which is a cut in the budget which gives money back to taxpayers in this country, it will not get through Parliament"' (BBC News 2012).

The defeat caused frustration within the Government, as it took some time to persuade the other 26 member states that the UK remained serious about the negotiations but in the end Parliament appeared vindicated, as the MFF did indeed see a real-terms reduction. Cameron certainly lost little opportunity to take the credit for having reduced the UK's contributions, and the 2015 Conservative Party Manifesto claimed that Labour 'gave away £7 billion of the British rebate ... We cut the EU budget for the first time ever, saving

British taxpayers £8.15 billion' (Conservative Party 2015, p. 72). The outcome would have been rather different, however, had there not been a strong group of states, including Germany, which sought to cap the EU budget at 1% of gross national income (GNI). As always, the outcomes of fraught EU negotiations owed something to a convergence of views, not just the demands of a single member state. Nonetheless, Cameron had secured a notable success. The words of Reckless were, however, to prove a foretaste of the fractious referendum debates in which the UK's contribution to the EU took centre stage, despite being capped at 1% of GNI, a bare fiftieth of national public spending.

European Democracy at Work: EP Elections 2014 and the Juncker Debacle

The 2014 EP elections were the first to take place under the provisions of the Lisbon Treaty; in accordance with these, the EP was to elect the Commission President, and the European Council was to take the results of the EP elections into consideration in nominating the candidate for that presidency. Thus the main EP party groups each put forward a candidate for Commission President, in the event of their group winning the most seats in the EP elections. The idea behind the Lisbon reforms was to elicit greater interest in EP elections and create a more direct link between the Commission and the peoples of Europe. In the vast majority of EU member states the logic could be made to work at least in principle: most states have parties that are members of the transnational political parties – the EPP, Party of European Socialists (PES), Alliance of Liberals and Democrats for Europe (ALDE), and the Greens – and the lead candidate or *Spitzenkandidat*, the German word which had gained currency, could thus serve as a focus for the campaigns. So at least the theory ran, although outside Germany and Luxembourg it did not really achieve the expectations of Europe's political élites in 2014. In the UK the whole idea fell flat: the Tories' withdrawal from the dominant EPP family ahead of the 2009 EP elections ensured the EPP did not feature in the UK campaign, other than in the London region, where a new grouping, the EPP-UK, did field a list of candidates. Nor did the lead candidates of the PES or ALDE feature in the British campaigns. The Labour leadership rejected the idea that sitting EP President and Socialist candidate Martin Schulz should visit the UK, believing his brand of pro-Europeanism would be unhelpful in the Eurosceptic British context. The Liberal Democrats had gone a stage further, formally recommending an abstention on the nomination of Guy Verhofstadt as the ALDE candidate, believing his federalist tendencies would be a liability, even though he was ALDE's only candidate following the withdrawal of the Liberal Democrats' preferred candidate, Finnish Commissioner Olli Rehn. The Conservatives and UKIP were both members of Eurosceptic groupings in the EP which did not nominate EU-wide lead candidates, so they naturally focused solely on the domestic level. Thus, none of the main UK parties engaged in moves to 'Europeanise' the European elections.

UK voters were kept apart from moves towards EU-level democracy, which arguably became a self-fulfilling matter. There cannot be democracy without a demos; remaining outside moves to create a demos ensures that one is unlikely ever to emerge. The focus in 2014, as in the past, was on national parties and national issues. In a context marked by years of austerity budgets and where the Liberal Democrats had lost their status as the 'UK protest party of choice', the way was paved for the Greens and, especially, UKIP to garner support – the Greens won three seats compared to the Liberal Democrats' one, while UKIP topped the poll, winning 24 seats to the Tories' 19, on 27.5% of the popular vote. The turnout was low, at 35.6%, but the message was clear: there was significant support for UKIP not just in traditionally Eurosceptic areas but right across England and Wales, a phenomenon that the Remain side perhaps failed to comprehend ahead of the referendum. The Tories' promise of a referendum might have prevented the party from splitting but it had not stopped the rise of UKIP. Meanwhile, Labour and the Liberal Democrats had sought to distance themselves from two figures who would in due course play key roles in EU negotiations and votes on Brexit – President of the EP Martin Schulz and EP rapporteur for Brexit, Guy Verhofstadt. The Conservatives were set to antagonise a third: Jean-Claude Juncker.

When the results of the EP elections were known, the two main party groups – the PES and EPP – immediately agreed that Juncker, as the EPP's nominee for Commission President, should be the chosen candidate to put to the European Parliament for 'election' in accordance with the provisions of the Lisbon Treaty. This proposal accorded with the fact that the EPP was the largest group in the EP and, while a case could have been made that since the group was far short of a majority in the EP, he would not automatically become President, the consensus between the two largest groups was to abide by the spirit of the Lisbon Treaty; a decision no doubt assisted by the fact that Schulz was most unusually granted a second term of office as President of the European Parliament.[5] This proposal was wholly unacceptable to David Cameron, however, and he swiftly sought to block the appointment of Juncker. However, the Lisbon Treaty had ensured that the decision would be taken by QMV, not unanimity. With only Hungarian PM Viktor Orban joining Cameron in a dissenting vote, the UK could not stop the nomination. His failure to block Juncker represented yet another example of Cameron's inability to play the European game: he did not have enough friends and had not prepared the ground adequately. Again, he was paying the price for taking his party out of the EPP – as a member he would have had a seat at the table when the centre-right chose Juncker to be the *Spitzenkandidat*. Had Cameron been present, perhaps a name other than Juncker's would have been put forward. Of course, this is one of the great unknowns. What was known was that after four years in office the UK was not playing the leading role that the coalition had pledged.

The failure to block Juncker was not a complete disaster from Cameron's perspective, even if it showed once more his failure to understand the rules of the European game: he could argue that he had sought to block a federalist Commission President and, hence, was acting in the national interest. For Conservatives worried about his Eurosceptic credentials, he was making the right noises even if he had failed to secure the right result. Yet from a European perspective this could be construed as yet another example of British 'awkwardness' – never in the right place at the right time, nor having prepared the ground correctly in advance of decisions being taken. To be sure, he had endeavoured to obtain the support of Angela Merkel and other key allies, including Dutch premier Mark Rutte and the then Swedish PM Fredrik Reinfeldt, but he neglected one crucial aspect of European politics: it is not only British politicians who have domestic constituencies, media, voters and parties to keep on board; so does every other EU leader. When they are in coalition as the vast majority are, it is even harder for leaders simply to give their British counterpart what he or she asks for. They may offer to do so in good faith but whether they will be able to deliver is another matter. Too often UK politicians and commentators seem to forget this simple but immutable aspect of European politics.

What was true in the nomination of the Commission President would be equally true for other matters on which Cameron sought movement: reform of the EU, including repatriation of powers, an end to 'ever closer union' and curbs on one of the EU's sacred cows, namely the free movement of people. A failure to give the UK what it demanded was not a sign of obduracy on the part of the 26 or 27 other member states, but an indication that for each and every member state national interests and domestic factors matter. The EU has not eliminated national interest nor in most areas usurped national sovereignty, regardless of what its detractors assert. Some things make it easier to secure one's objectives, however, and having a strong network of partners on whom one can broadly rely is one of them. This was one aspect of European politics to which Margaret Thatcher was wholly oblivious, while Tony Blair broadly understood it but failed to back up a generally constructive approach with the necessary reciprocity on which deals within the EU crucially depend. Cameron had perhaps modelled himself rather too much on Thatcher in this regard, even if he played his hand well in the MFF negotiations. His attempts at bilateralism relied too much on relations with Chancellor Merkel at the expense of a wider, durable network of allies, making it hard for him to achieve key objectives at crucial moments in EU negotiations – a lesson that he needed to learn ahead of the reforms that he had pledged to negotiate in the event of being re-elected in 2015.

Notes

1 The Liberal Democrats were only formed in 1988 following the merger of the Liberals and the Social Democrat Party, so had technically never been in government as their Liberal forebears had been.
2 I am grateful to Michael Steed for making this point on various occasions.
3 The source for all the quotations in this paragraph is HM Government (2010), p. 19.
4 Conservative MP Bob Neill topped the ballot for PMBs the following year and proposed a similar bill to Wharton's, but it made even less progress.
5 The President of the EP is appointed at the start of the new Parliament for two and a half years and normally replaced by a candidate from another party for the second half of the Parliament. The role has generally alternated between candidates from the PES and the EPP, with ALDE occasionally securing a turn.

6 Cameron's Three Rs
Reform, renegotiation, referendum

David Cameron would need all his negotiating skills to deliver the 'three Rs' – reform, renegotiation and referendum – that he had pledged at Bloomberg and which underpinned the Conservatives' electoral promises in subsequent elections. Only one of the three, the referendum itself, would be wholly within his control, and that only if the Conservatives won an outright majority in the 2015 general election. Reform of the EU and renegotiating the UK's terms of membership would require agreement from all 27 other member states as well as the European Parliament. The chances of a Conservative majority government seemed slim and some suggested that it was the fact he did not expect to win the election, certainly not outright, that emboldened Cameron to make his Bloomberg pledge in the first place. In the event, the Conservatives won a narrow majority of twelve and Cameron was thus required to deliver on his promises to renegotiate and hold an 'in/out' referendum by the end of 2017. His carefully constructed timeframe for a meaningful negotiation and the promised 'time for a proper, reasoned debate' (Cameron 2013) quickly unravelled as he sought to go to the country as early as possible, namely in June 2016, a decision that truncated both his negotiations and the campaign to remain in the EU. The renegotiation was based on a watered-down version of the Bloomberg commitments, which had reflected the perennial themes of sovereignty and the euro (and the UK's position outside the eurozone) with the addition of a new theme: immigration.

The Calm before the Storm

The 2013 'Bloomberg speech' served Cameron well for two and a half years. It provided a nod to the importance of the European project and a sufficiently constructive tone to secure support from the more Europhile among his party, while giving the sceptics the prospect of change – whether through reform or the chance to leave. The upshot was that he had bought himself time. The European question did not go away, but for the rest of the Parliament his party was able to coalesce around the 'three Rs'. In addition to enabling him to hold his party together through the 2014 EP elections and the 2015 general election, Cameron's approach allowed the Conservatives to distinguish themselves from all their rivals. Only the Conservatives would offer a referendum on EU membership, they claimed: Labour and the Liberal Democrats would not, and UKIP could not (Conservative Party 2014; Conservative Party 2015). While this was somewhat misleading regarding their coalition partners, given the Liberal Democrats' long-standing calls for an 'in/out' referendum, albeit at the time of treaty reform, the general thrust of the Tory position was clear. If you believed that the UK needed a referendum on the vexed European question, then only the Conservatives could and would deliver it; UKIP was too electorally insignificant, at least at the national level.

The EU featured extensively in the Scottish independence referendum of September 2014. The case for Scotland leaving the United Kingdom was predicated on Scotland remaining a member of the EU after breaking away from the rest of the UK. Thus the SNP-led 'Yes' campaign supporting independence claimed that an independent Scotland could be in the EU, but outside the UK. The 'Better Together' campaign, which brought together the three main Unionist parties – Conservative, Labour and the Liberal Democrats – argued that there was no guarantee that Scotland would automatically be permitted to remain in the EU. While there was no precedent for a member state splitting up, it seemed that such a scenario would require the departing entity to request membership. Whether or not that would be considered as a wholly new application in the way a 'third country' application would be was unclear, but it seemed unlikely that a country which already met the EU's membership criteria through existing membership as part of a member state would be subjected to the sort of protracted negotiations normally associated with the accession process. Yet it was known that some existing member states, notably Spain, anxious to avoid a precedent that could give further oxygen to the secessionist Catalans, would seek to block any such moves. The Commission President also announced that the 'rump UK' rather than Scotland would benefit from the rights of being the continuing member state. 'Project Fear', which saw Labour and the Liberal Democrats working with the Conservatives to secure a 'no' vote and which benefited from strong media support, prevailed; Scotland voted to stay within the UK. However, the referendum had created bitter divisions within the country, which would have significant ramifications in the general election and the EU referendum.

The Tories continued their truce through the general election of May 2015, when a similar line was taken on the EU as in the 2014 EP elections. The party made an unequivocal commitment to holding 'an in-out referendum by the end of 2017'. They could only deliver on this promise if they won the election, which the polls suggested they would not. Indeed, the confident expectation of most commentators and many politicians was that there would be another hung parliament, necessitating either minority government or a further coalition. The chances of Cameron ever having to deliver the proposed 'three Rs' looked remote. After all, surely the Liberal Democrats would make the referendum a red line in any second coalition agreement, or so some may have hoped. However, the ruthless renewal of Project Fear in England, with a campaign directed by Lynton Crosby pressing the dangers of a Labour-led coalition government dancing to the tune of the SNP, resulted in the vast majority of their erstwhile Liberal Democrat colleagues losing their seats. Moreover, the electoral system ensured that UKIP, with four million votes, only retained one parliamentary seat; this, coupled with the dramatic SNP landslide in Scotland where it won 56 out of 59 seats, meant that the unexpected happened. The Conservatives were returned to office as a single-party administration with a clear, albeit small majority. Finally the stage was set for UK citizens to be asked their thoughts about membership of the EU, forty years after that 1975 poll which had endorsed ongoing membership of the Community by a majority of two to one.

The time had come for David Cameron to deliver on his 'three Rs' pledge. The reality would prove harder than the rhetoric. Cameron had chosen a high-stakes, high-risk strategy, putting the UK's membership of the EU on the line largely for reasons of internal party management. He now needed to persuade the other 27 EU member states – and his own party – that he was serious in his intention to secure reform and new terms of membership. For the other 27 there was also a need to demonstrate the UK's commitment to the EU: after all, the rhetoric from the UK was increasingly sceptic, particularly with the presence of UKIP leader Nigel Farage in the EP, reflecting the rise of popular Euroscepticism. 'If the UK is already in the departure lounge, why should we bother?' some member states wondered. Nor would demands for asymmetric reforms intended only for the UK be acceptable for leaders facing domestic challenges of their own. Meanwhile, superficial changes would not be acceptable to many in Cameron's own party who were minded to support campaigns to leave the EU, but had not finally made up their minds.

In the six months following the general election, David Cameron began to explore a package of possible requests with his EU partners. Like British politicians, they kept asserting that they did not know what Cameron wanted, because he refused to set anything down on paper until he had clarity on what would be achievable. In practice the demands were similar to those originally outlined at Bloomberg and in the Conservative general election manifesto: non-discrimination between eurozone and non-eurozone countries; 'sovereignty', understood as enhanced powers for national parliaments, greater emphasis on subsidiarity and agreement that the UK would no longer be bound by the doctrine of 'ever closer union'; competitiveness – linked to the internal market and reducing regulation; and 'welfare' in terms of minimising the scope for EU nationals to claim various welfare benefits immediately upon arrival in the UK. These demands were formally outlined by the UK PM in a letter of 10 November 2015 to Donald Tusk, President of the European Council.

Preparing for a Referendum

Moves to hold a referendum commenced as early as the Queen's Speech immediately following the general election, as Cameron sought to demonstrate his commitment to holding the promised referendum by the end of 2017.[1] Legislation was introduced into the House of Commons in June 2015. Whereas the legislation for the 1975 referendum had been completed in great haste **after** the renegotiation had been completed, in 2015 the Government initiated the referendum legislation alongside starting informal discussions with the other member states about the possibilities for reform and renegotiation. Thus, there was time for thorough scrutiny of the draft legislation, which had to be framed in the context of the Political Parties, Elections and Referendums Act 2000 (PPERA). The intention of that Act was to create a level playing field in referendums, ensuring that neither side would be disadvantaged (the assumption being that a referendum would offer a binary choice rather than multiple options). Thus, the legislation proposed in 2015 needed to be placed in a more formal and heavily regulated framework than had been the case forty years previously.

PPERA had created a requirement for 'purdah', a set period in the run-up to an election or referendum during which the government and other public bodies are not permitted to campaign. The Government initially sought to argue that purdah should not apply to the proposed EU referendum, with Foreign Secretary Philip Hammond claiming both that it would prevent the UK engaging in its day-to-day EU business and that the Government would clearly want to be able to sell its deal once negotiated (HC Deb 9 June 2015, Col. 1055). MPs from all sides opposed this line and the Government was defeated on the matter: purdah would apply in the month prior to the poll. The Referendum Bill made provisions for designating two umbrella organisations, one each for the Remain and Leave campaigns, as well as setting caps on expenditure for these organisations, other permitted participants and political parties. While the two umbrella organisations would be given equal state resources (£600,000), rights to televised referendum broadcasts and a referendum communication delivered to every household/elector; each would have a spending limit of £7m. – parliamentarians on the Leave side expressed considerable frustration that the Remain campaign had a significant advantage: Labour, the Liberal Democrats and the Greens were all formally committed to Remain and could easily outspend the only party supporting Leave, namely UKIP, as the Conservatives were formally neutral, meaning neither side would be able to utilise that party's spending cap. As with many aspects of the referendum, MPs and peers, particularly on the Leave side, rehearsed their arguments during the passage of the European Union Referendum Act 2015 and it was obvious that they would cry foul at any apparent unfairness in the campaign. Such cries would not be long in coming, not least over the Government's role.

The recommendations of the Electoral Commission on the formulation of the question were accepted, that the most impartial way of framing the question to put to the voters was 'Should the United Kingdom remain a member of the European Union or leave the European Union?', with voters invited to indicate 'Remain a member of the European Union' or 'Leave the European Union'. The question was somewhat cumbersome as it was intended to avoid a straight 'yes/no' answer, which is thought by some to favour the positive 'yes' side. The word 'remain' was needed, since the Commission had previously found some people were not aware that the UK was already a member of the EU. The balance was, perhaps, in favour of those who wanted to withdraw from the EU: 'remain' is a stale word, lacking the dynamic element of 'leave', and the Leavers would use the dynamism to good effect.

There was extensive debate about the scope of the franchise as Labour, Liberal Democrats and the cross-benchers (independents or members of minor parties) sought to enfranchise 16 and 17 year olds, as the Scottish Government had done in the independence referendum of 2014. After repeated parliamentary votes, the Government's preference for retaining 18 as the minimum age for voting prevailed, unbending to the Opposition's argument that it was young people who would suffer the consequences for longer than anyone else. Nor was the Government willing to allow EU nationals resident in the UK or UK nationals resident in other EU countries for more than 15 years to vote. Each of these proposed extensions to the franchise would have had the merit of giving a say to those people who stood to be significantly affected by the outcome of the referendum. EU nationals resident in the UK and UK residents elsewhere in the EU were, after all, European citizens actively exercising their rights of citizenship, including free movement. That all three groups were likely to favour Remain over Leave ensured that those on the Leave side argued strenuously against such proposed changes and Remainers were somewhat handicapped in making the case by the fact that they could not refute the criticism that their proposed alterations to the franchise would benefit them electorally. The upshot was that the electorate rather bizarrely included Commonwealth citizens resident in the UK, no matter how short their residency had been or was expected to be, but not EU nationals. The exceptions were that Cypriots and Maltese citizens were also able to vote, being Commonwealth citizens in addition to being EU nationals. Citizens of Gibraltar were enfranchised, as they are in elections to the EP.

Members of the House of Lords devoted much effort to try to persuade the Government to produce objective information on what leaving the EU would look like, as they had demanded during the Wharton PMB two years earlier. The Minister concerned, Baroness Anelay of St Johns, was remarkably resistant, repeatedly insisting that it was up to those who advocated Leave to say what Leave would look like. Eventually, a compromise was reached, with the Government agreeing to produce a white paper on the eventual outcome of the renegotiation and its recommendations as well as documents on the alternatives to membership and the 'rights and responsibilities of membership', a proxy for a report on the 'consequences of withdrawal'. When the documents were finally produced in late February and March 2016 they were greeted with something between disdain and incredulity by the Leavers, who referred to the White Paper as 'propaganda' (HL Deb 2 March 2016, Col. 834). The other promised documents also lacked the sort of rigour and objectivity needed to be of value to the public in the referendum. It was only as weeks and months passed after the referendum that it became clear why there was such reluctance to produce objective information on what leaving might look like: the Government had simply not done the work; they did not expect to lose the referendum and, hence, had made no preparations for that eventuality. The nature of the reports and the Remain side's overall complacency did not augur well for the referendum. Quite how ill prepared they were was not so evident at the time.

Reform and Renegotiation

The commitment to a referendum by the end of 2017 was shaped by domestic and European factors and reflected the desire to have a sufficient amount of time for renegotiating the UK's terms of membership. It was intended to provide the longest period for negotiations any time before 2020, taking into consideration the UK general elections due in 2015 and 2020 alongside the French Presidential elections due in mid-2017, German Federal elections in autumn 2017 and the fact that the UK was due to hold the rotating Presidency of the European Council in the second half of 2017. The expectation was thus that, if re-elected as Prime Minister, Cameron would take up to two years to negotiate suitable changes, ideally holding a referendum in May 2017 before the UK took on the Presidency. This would not give sufficient time for any reforms requiring treaty change, which immediately ensured that those in his party and beyond who sought fundamental reform would be unlikely to be satisfied by the outcome. It became clear shortly after the election that he was hoping to hold the referendum by summer 2016 in order both to avoid having yet another Conservative Party conference overshadowed by divisions over the EU and lest public opinion be affected by a recurrence of the previous year's refugee crisis, which saw hundreds of people dying in the Mediterranean. Nonetheless, he told European Council President Donald Tusk in his first formal letter outlining his demands for reform on 10 November 2015 that, 'It remains my aim to conclude an agreement at the earliest opportunity, but the priority is to get the substance right'.

The fact that both his sceptical backbenchers and his EU interlocutors were aware of his impatience to secure a deal perhaps left him less able to leverage the best deal he could have done. Moreover, while his four 'baskets' or areas of reform – Economic Governance; Competitiveness; Sovereignty; and Immigration – matched the Bloomberg agenda quite closely plus the addition of immigration, there was a watering down of demands, certainly as far as Tory manifestos were concerned. The four areas reflected the UK's perennial concerns about sovereignty, the single market and the eurozone as well as the more recent concern about immigration or, more accurately in the context of the EU, free movement of people. However, while the ambition was to 'under-promise and over-deliver' (source: off-the-record interview), the reverse proved to be the case, as expectations were raised on the extent to which reform might be achievable.

In its 2014 Manifesto for the EP elections, the Conservative Party (2014, p. 28) had offered a far-reaching set of commitments, including the lines:

> 'If you want our country to keep control of its own borders
> 'Vote Conservative
> 'If you want to keep Britain out of eurozone bailouts
> 'Vote Conservative
> 'If you want to take back control of criminal justice
> 'Vote Conservative.'

In his introduction to that manifesto, Cameron rehearsed many of the themes of his Bloomberg Speech, which would form part not of **his** narrative in the referendum but rather that of his Leave opponents: 'I hear time and again from people about their frustrations with the EU: it is too bureaucratic and too undemocratic. It interferes too much in our daily lives, and the scale of EU migration triggered by new members joining in recent years has had a huge impact on local communities' (Conservative Party 2014, p. 5). The Conservatives were keen to pledge action on immigration – not an EU matter *per se* but one that had become increasingly intertwined in the Conservative-UKIP discourse. There was a clear recognition of the importance of free movement of workers, as had been provided for in the Treaty of Rome, but a rejection of 'benefit tourism and abuse' (Conservative Party 2014, p. 14). It was never stated how much abuse there actually was, but this became a key part of discussions for the next two years, running through the renegotiation and referendum, perhaps because the Conservatives were so keen to flag it as an issue. They pledged to 'Press for a return to free movement of **workers**; free movement is a central principle of the EU, but it cannot be a freedom to move just for more generous benefits' (Conservative Party 2014, p. 14; emphasis added). In addition, they pledged to seek changes to the rights of EU citizens to claim benefits, something which would eventually become a key plank of the renegotiation. On 28 November 2014, Cameron (2014) made a major speech on immigration in which he said that 'immigration benefits Britain, but it needs to be controlled.' Aware of the pressures of immigration in some UK communities, he argued, as his predecessor Michael Howard had done in the 2005 general election, that: 'It is not wrong to express concern about the scale of people coming into the country. People have understandably become frustrated. It boils down to one word: control' (Cameron 2014). That one word, 'control' would prove to be crucial in the struggle to hold the UK in the EU.

While Cameron went on to present a far more nuanced approach to immigration, the concerns and desire for control resonated with UK voters, as the events of June 2016 demonstrated. The Conservatives had raised expectations on which they would not be able to deliver. The 2014 EP election manifesto and Cameron's 2014 speech both heightened expectations and used language that would become the staple of the Vote Leave campaign, that the UK should 'keep control of its own borders' and 'take back control'. Cameron (2014) asserted: ' ... freedom of movement itself is not an absolute. There are rules for when new member states join the EU precisely to cope with excessive numbers. So why can't there be steps to allow member states a greater degree of control ... ?' The 2015 manifesto had pledged to bring net migration down to 'the tens of thousands, not hundreds of thousands' and to 'control migration from the European Union' – though it added the caveat 'by reforming welfare rules' (Conservative Party 2015, p. 29). The expectation had been raised that immigration would be reduced; the small print and the niceties of EU rules, by contrast, were rather neglected.

Thus, when his letter to Tusk was published, many backbenchers expressed their amazement and disappointment at the limited nature of Cameron's requests. In 2015, the Conservative Manifesto had pledged 'Real change in our relationship with the European Union ... No to "ever closer union". No to a constant flow of power to Brussels. No to unnecessary interference. And no, of course, to the Euro, to participation in eurozone bail-outs or notions like a European Army.' (Conservative Party 2015, p. 72.) In fact, the MFF deal in 2013 had already reduced the 'cost of Europe', and the Economic Governance and Competitiveness 'baskets' did tackle the questions about British business and the importance of 'non-discrimination' for non-eurozone countries. Requests in the context of the 'Immigration' basket were limited, focusing mainly on benefits tourism and the somewhat disconnected matter of 'sham' marriages, rather than asking for any more fundamental revisions to free movement rules. No request was made for a return to free movement of 'workers' as proposed in the Conservatives' 2015 manifesto. Given the huge significance other member states pay to free movement of people, this was perhaps not surprising.

The Maastricht Treaty's change from 'free movement of labour' to 'free movement of people' had ensured there was a sense in the UK that people were coming not just to work and were putting pressure on services, including housing, school places and hospital beds, all of which contributed to a growing alienation from the EU and even in some cases against EU nationals. The *quid pro quo* of millions of UK nationals living, working and, especially, retiring to other EU countries thanks to these self-same rights of free movement received far less attention. The impact at home was what mattered to Cameron, to those who campaigned to leave the EU and to the voters, but there was little that the UK could reasonably expect to change, given the nature of a single market that it had itself done so much to foster. The free movement of people was an issue that would come back to haunt the Government after the vote to leave the EU.

The reactions of Eurosceptics were blunt: Bill Cash queried 'How is the PM going to sell this pig in a poke?' (HC Deb 10 Nov 2015, Col. 229); Jacob Rees-Mogg remarked that 'the list makes Harold Wilson's renegotiation look respectable' (HC Deb 10 Nov 2015, Col. 232), while Bernard Jenkin wondered, 'Is that it?' (HC Deb 10 Nov 2015, Col. 236). Clearly Cameron's renegotiation was not going to reconcile the irreconcilables. Indeed, it was inevitable that confirmed Eurosceptics would not and could not be placated by a renegotiation short of full reform, and this list fell short of full reform. What was less clear was whether there would be enough to win over those genuinely wavering, waiting to see the deal the PM would bring back.

Over the course of three months, the Government sought to negotiate on the rather limited prospectus. Cameron requested the backing of his MPs during the renegotiation and it was expected that MPs would not declare their views on membership until the outcome of the renegotiation was known; failure to do so would weaken both Cameron's leadership and his negotiating hand. However, in early January 2016 he announced that MPs and indeed ministers would be allowed to campaign as they saw fit; collective responsibility would be waived, as it had been in 1975. The starting gun had been fired for an impassioned intra-Conservative battle over the EU which would be played out in public.

When the outcome of the renegotiation was announced after months of informal and then formal talks with EU partners, culminating in a two-day European summit meeting in mid-February 2016, Cameron hailed the deal as being sufficient to allow him to recommend to the Cabinet that the Government should support remaining in the EU. Scarcely a 'reformed EU' – Cameron had not allowed himself or his EU partners time for genuine reform – the deal did nonetheless provide some concessions for the UK. Indeed, Cameron was quick to stress the 'special status' that the UK had been granted by the renegotiation (see HM Government 2016). Two aspects were particularly significant in that regard: firstly, an agreement that the UK would no longer be bound by the principle of 'ever-closer union' and hence would not be tied to political integration; and, secondly, a decision to drop the commitment to the euro being the only EU currency in the long term, with associated policy changes to ensure that non-eurozone countries like the UK would not be discriminated against in trading within the single market – a key concession for the City of London. There were other 'sovereignty' concessions including strengthening of the rights on national parliaments, as well as commitments to the third of Cameron's baskets: competitiveness. The immigration/free movement agreement was a rather limited one relating to benefits and sham marriages, falling far short of the commitments that Cameron and the Conservatives had been making in the previous couple of years. In this area, above all, the Government had over-promised and under-delivered; at least as far as those seeking a reduction in the numbers of EU nationals moving to live in the UK were concerned. The agreement would be lodged at the United Nations and be justiciable under international, not EU, law at such time as the UK voted to remain in the EU. In the event of a vote to leave the EU, the agreement would fall.

The Battle Lines are Drawn

Cameron convened a Cabinet meeting the morning after the European Council meeting, recommending that the deal be accepted and that the Government should support the UK remaining in the EU. The majority of the Cabinet backed him. In line with the agreement to waive collective responsibility on the matter, five full Cabinet members – Michael Gove (Secretary of State for Justice), Iain Duncan Smith (Secretary of State for Work and Pensions), Chris Grayling (Leader of the House of Commons), John Whittingdale (Secretary of State for Culture, Media and Sport) and Theresa Villiers (Secretary of State for Northern Ireland) – along with Priti Patel, who attended Cabinet as Minister of State for Employment, declared they were advocating leaving the EU. Barely had Cameron announced the Cabinet's decision to support remaining than the six appeared at the Vote Leave headquarters, making the divisions within Government all too apparent.

While most of those campaigning to leave were long-standing critics of the EU, the decision of Michael Gove to support Leave came as a shock personal betrayal to David Cameron, who believed he had an assurance of support from his old friend, whichever way Cameron came down on the argument (Walters 2016, p. 1). Also surprising in terms of her Cabinet role was the decision of Theresa Villiers to campaign to leave the EU. She was a known Eurosceptic but the situation in Northern Ireland and the question of relations with the Republic both stood to be profoundly affected by a decision to leave the EU – something that Villiers and other Leavers sought strenuously to play down, arguing that there had been no hard border between Northern Ireland and the Republic before, and so there was no reason why there would have to be one if the UK left the EU. This was a neat line of argument, albeit one that ignored the fact that since Irish independence both countries had either been outside the EU or both inside, so the question of external EU borders between the two countries had never arisen; the Leavers' preferred outcome was without precedent. Coupled with the fact that the Leave campaign was arguing to reduce free movement of people, the UK-Irish passport union seemed at risk, since it would be impossible to monitor the movement of other EU nationals coming into Northern Ireland from the Republic and thence into the rest of the UK if there were no passport controls.

Of greater concern to the Remain campaign was the decision by former Mayor of London, and one of the Conservatives' most popular politicians, Boris Johnson, to support Leave. Through his regular column in *The Daily Telegraph*, Johnson had urged Cameron to demonstrate his willingness to leave the EU in order to secure the best deal during the renegotiation. Yet, despite his scepticism about the EU, this suggestion seemed like sound negotiating advice, not a call to leave. The expectation was that Johnson would come down for Remain and he even penned two alternative articles immediately after the renogotiation, one supporting Remain and one Leave, only deciding at the last minute that it would be the Leave case that he published (the Remain case was subsequently published in the *Sunday Times* on 16 October 2016). This last-minute decision was a severe blow for the Remain side. Whereas in 1975 those arguing to leave the Common Market could quite easily be dismissed as marginal figures, remote from the political mainstream, the Leave campaign of 2016 was shaping up rather differently.

The Leavers would argue that Remain had all the advantages, not least the weight of the Government machine until the purdah period kicked in a month before the referendum date. Yet, in practice the Leave campaign benefited from the passion and energy that the Remainers seemed to lack, with an emotional message that resonated with voters, and the ability to use an anti-establishment card that served them well throughout the referendum campaign, not to mention support from the bulk of the print media. Moreover, they were able to tap into an anti-immigration sentiment that the Remain camp seemed unable to counter. Critically, they adopted a narrative of 'control' that David Cameron himself had been using just months before.

The Referendum Itself

The referendum offered a binary choice: remain or leave. Yet the issue at stake was complex, the alternatives to membership never fully articulated, and the far-reaching implications of a vote to leave never fully clarified by its proponents. David Cameron had pledged to hold an 'in/out' referendum, language which would have resonated with ordinary people. A 'yes/no' approach would also have been relatively straightforward, in line with the wording used in 1975 and in most EU treaty ratification referendums in other member states, notably Ireland and Denmark. However, the Electoral Commission's recommended wording ensured the status quo option of 'Remain' sounded rather static compared with the alternative: 'Leave'. In accordance with the legislation, the Electoral Commission designated two cross-party umbrella campaign groups, Britain Stronger in Europe (the only applicant) for Remain and Vote Leave for the Leave campaign.

Not only did 'leave' have the advantage of apparent dynamism, it was also used rather effectively by the Leave campaigners. The name of the umbrella leave organisation could be considered an order or an exhortation: vote [to] leave. The citizen so persuaded could then be expected to go to the polling station and do just that – put a cross against the option 'Leave the European Union'. Those advocating staying in European Union were rather hampered by the dull word 'remain', which was not even in the title of the umbrella remain organisation: Britain Stronger in Europe or BSE. The main focus was on the word 'In' and BSE was registered as such; remain was nowhere to be seen. Indeed, the official BSE campaign was launched on 12 October before the formal wording of the question had been definitively agreed, but at that stage the Electoral Commission's recommendation was already clear and it would presumably have been possible to have rebranded the campaign ahead of the launch. An alternative name would have been advantageous for another reason. The abbreviation of BSE was an unfortunate reminder of that other BSE – 'mad cow disease' – which had dogged the dying days of John Major's premiership.

BSE was not only hampered by its unfortunate name. Fronting the campaign at least from its launch until post-renegotiation, when it was expected that the Prime Minister would take the lead, was Lord Rose. Rose, former Chairman and CEO of Marks and Spencer, had previously been a member of the Eurosceptic Business for Britain. While Rose did accept the case for the UK's ongoing membership of the EU, his appointment to lead the key Remain campaign was nonetheless a strange one. A late convert to the European cause **after** the PM had achieved his renegotiation might have been able to argue very effectively for their new cause and make the case to undecided voters that the deal had persuaded them to vote Remain and encourage waverers to do likewise. But the choice of a latecomer to the European cause to lead the whole campaign was more perplexing, and in his gaffe-prone interventions in the campaign Rose never displayed the necessary zeal of the convert. His comment at the launch that each family benefited by £480 million from EU membership (others would have dropped the million!) suggested he was totally out of touch with ordinary families, and he repeatedly got BSE's name wrong, leading to much parody. By the end of the campaign he had vanished from public display.

The Campaigns

Funded initially by Lord Sainsbury and subsequently benefiting from funding from Goldman Sachs, BSE brought together leading figures from the main political parties, including former EU Commissioner Peter Mandelson, former Chief Secretary to the Treasury Danny Alexander and former Minister of State for Immigration Damian Green, along with Andrew Cooper, founder of the Populus opinion polling company, and Ryan Coetzee, who had been Director of Strategy for the Liberal Democrats in their notably unsuccessful 2015 General Election campaign. The expectation, however, was that once the renegotiation was complete David Cameron would lead the Remain campaign, not least given his commitment to campaigning 'heart and soul' to keep the UK in the EU. In practice, Cameron's role was a mixed blessing. His determination to avoid 'blue on blue' conflict led him to refuse to debate against either Michael Gove or Boris Johnson, the two leading Conservative Leavers. He also refused to sanction a powerful last-minute advertising campaign by Saatchi & Saatchi, which was deemed to be too 'personal' (Elliott 2016). Moreover, the dominant BSE strategy was one that privileged 'pocket-book economics' over other issues. The assumption was that, just as (some) Scottish voters were believed to have been won over to the Better Together cause by the perceived economic costs to them of leaving the UK, so voters undecided about the EU question would be won over by the costs to them of leaving the EU. This narrow economic focus proved far less effective in the Brexit context, as voters were won over by arguments that touched the heart at least as much as the head. This was partly because few actually believed the figures the Treasury put out seeking to model very precisely what each household would lose by 2030. Given the Treasury's normal inability to predict accurately six months ahead, these attempts stretched credulity and the predictions failed to resonate before the referendum, being characterised by Leavers as part of 'Project Fear'.

Identity politics mattered. Vote Leave's compellingly simple message of 'taking back control' understood this. For citizens who felt left behind by globalisation and European integration, the idea of 'taking back control' appeared to offer a way out of the situation into which they had fallen, through no choice of their own. As with those supporting the *Front National* in France, some of those supporting Leave felt that leaving the EU would be a way to allow them to reshape their future. Coupled with a strong narrative on immigration, Vote Leave was able to tap into concerns that had arisen after decades of liberal immigration policy, coupled with increasingly large numbers of EU citizens exercising their treaty-based rights to move to the UK after the 'big bang' enlargement. No longer restricted to free movement of labour this shift had over the years contributed to public frustrations, which, as shown above, had carefully been cultivated by the Conservative Party, with manifestos calling for immigration to be brought down to 'tens of thousands'. EU policies adopted by Labour and accepted by the Conservatives, and vice versa, had contributed to a situation where in 2016 voters blamed the EU for many perceived ills, even though in most cases the changes had come about at the behest of, or with the active support of, the UK. BSE simply had no tools in its armoury to respond effectively.

The Parties' Campaigns

BSE expected the main political parties to inject a passion into the Remain campaign that its own activities lacked. The parties ran individual 'In' campaigns. The hope was that Labour, the Liberal Democrats, the Greens and the pro-EU part of the Conservative party would all mobilise their own supporters to secure the core 'remain' vote, which the umbrella BSE campaign was not targeting, with its focus on swing voters. By contrast, the Vote Leave campaign spoke to all potential Leavers, its campaign benefiting from a single narrative that could embrace the most Eurosceptic and persuade waverers. The Remain campaigners' messages were blurred and there was no over-arching narrative. The stronger, safer, more secure arguments (alongside exhortations not to take the risk of leaving, which was portrayed as 'a leap in the dark') worked only up to a point and failed to inspire many pro-Europeans, with whom a passionate peace narrative clearly resonated when they were exposed to it, but which they rarely encountered.

There were myriad reasons why someone might be pro-EU or be persuaded to vote Remain, including, peace, prosperity, environmental policy, the opportunity to study, work or retire elsewhere in the EU as well as workers' rights and mutual recognition of qualifications, but few of these points were articulated regularly or reliably by Remainers. Indeed, many of those formally recommending that the UK remain in the EU seemed to be 'reluctant Remainers' at best, spending time saying 'the EU's not perfect, but ... ', which was scarcely compelling. Despite the fact that the Remain campaign appeared to hold all the cards at the start of the campaign, including more money and the machinery of government, it quickly became clear that this was not enough. As the Government published its 'guidance' to every household in early April, at a reported cost of £9m., the Leave Campaign cried 'foul': taxpayers' money should not be spent putting the Government's pro-EU case. The media rapidly added oxygen to their objections; perversely, the £9m. gave added momentum to the Leave campaign, partly by ensuring it received a massive amount of free publicity and partly because the Government's action rendered it so much easier for those fundraising for Vote Leave to turn to potential donors and make the case that 'the Establishment is against us' (source: off-the-record conversations). Money flowed into the Leave campaign, as the regular donation reports published by the Electoral Commission made abundantly clear.

The Conservatives' part in the referendum was persistently overshadowed by splits in the party and the prospect of a leadership election. Regardless of the outcome of the referendum, David Cameron had made clear at the 2015 general election that he would not fight another election as leader; the race was on for his successor. If Tory MPs were unwilling to discuss the matter, the media were only too happy to look at the key figures on both sides of the referendum for their leadership potential rather more than the intrinsic merits of their case for or against EU membership. It was coverage neither Cameron nor the Remain campaign needed. Nor was the Labour contribution to the Remain campaign more noticeably successful, as leader of Labour In for Britain, former Home Secretary Alan Johnson, failed to make much impression on the airwaves, although he was apparently active in rallying the Labour faithful at meetings around the country. Party leader Jeremy Corbyn – the self-same Islington MP whom No. 10 had pointed out was one of the most Eurosceptic MPs in 1997 – was seen by many in his own party to be insufficiently passionate about remaining in the EU. Certainly, he was not at the forefront of any debates, unlike the incoming Labour Mayor of London, Sadiq Khan, who made a passionate case for Remain. The Liberal Democrats were resolutely positive and proactive in the campaign but there was little they could do to secure the sort of media coverage that might have helped them win significant numbers of voters over to Remain.

Meanwhile in Scotland the SNP campaigned strongly for a Remain vote, against the arguments of those – unionists and nationalists alike – who suggested that Scotland could never achieve true independence within the EU. However the SNP, like other mainstream parties supporting Remain, had put its campaigning focus on 5 May 2016, when the Scottish parliamentary elections were held, focusing on the referendum only after that date. Turnout was lower in Scotland than elsewhere in the referendum, giving rise to a sense that this had not been the main campaign of the year. The exhaustion, apathy, complacency, or whatever else may have engendered the mismatch in passion and activism in the two sides of the campaign reflected the sense that for Leavers 23 June was the only date that mattered, and had been for some time. The decision to bring the referendum forward was perhaps unwise, as the SNP had argued when the PM proposed a June poll (HC Deb 9 February 2016).

Vote Leave

The official Leave campaign had a simple message which spoke to a range of themes that had characterised British caution about the EU for decades: 'take back control', whether of our borders, money, trade, laws or democracy. Some of the themes were integral to the nature of the EU, some were actively fostered by the EU; several had been framed by David Cameron over the years, namely sovereignty, democracy, the EU budget, freedom of movement and enlargement. The UK's place in the world, including relations with the Commonwealth, also mattered to a campaign anxious to prove it had global concerns.

Laws, Courts, Sovereignty and Democracy

One aspect of European integration that caused concern among Leavers was the role of courts, notably the Court of Justice of the EU (CJEU) as the European Court was officially known after Lisbon. While the supremacy of Community law was in place when the UK joined, the sheer scope of European legislation had expanded and with it the scope of the Court's jurisdiction. Norman Lamont (2016) argued, 'In the 1970s, people were always conscious of sovereignty as an issue but the supremacy of EC law applied in a very limited area of economic law.' For those seeking to reaffirm national sovereignty and, especially parliamentary sovereignty, the interference of courts was anathema. One example was the fact that Scotland was being prevented by the courts from introducing minimum alcohol pricing, deprived of the right to implement its own policies in line with its government's manifesto (Johnson 2016); a vote to leave the EU would free Scotland from the clutches of the CJEU, it was suggested. Outside the EU, the UK would be free to set its own laws. Parliament would again be sovereign. Decisions would once again be wholly democratic – or so the argument went.

For Leavers whose main concern was sovereignty, including Bill Cash and Labour co-chair of the Vote Leave campaign, Gisela Stuart, what mattered was whether or not it was possible for citizens to vote out the people who make their laws. In a sovereign democratic nation state that is clearly possible. In the EU it is not. Those advocating Remain argued, with equal justification, that the EU was democratic, thanks to a directly elected Parliament which represents the citizens of Europe and the fact that the Council of Ministers and European Council comprise elected politicians representing the member states. Moreover, since the Lisbon Treaty, there is a clear process for appointing the President of the European Commission on the basis of the results of the EP elections. So an emergent democracy was in place. In reality, however, there was little public awareness of the workings of the EU or its democratic credentials, or otherwise. Years of neglect by the British media had ensured that few would have followed European affairs, certainly not the EP in any detail. The regular *Eurobarometer* polls regularly showed UK citizens to be among the least well informed about the EU, and repeated attempts by the EU to come closer to the citizens had paradoxically had the reverse effect, as citizens became ever more disaffected (Blair 2010, p. 538). 'Take back control of your laws', the Leavers called; 'The EU is democratic', was all the Remainers could reply: scarcely an inspiration to voters.

Free Movement of People

Three interrelated issues – free movement of people, immigration, and asylum – formed one of the most sensitive and effective parts of the Leave campaign. The Conservatives had long pledged to reduce net migration figures to the tens of thousands. When they took office in coalition with the Liberal Democrats in 2010 it became apparent that this pledge would be extremely difficult to deliver, given that there was no way of curtailing the numbers of EU migrants seeking to come to live and work in the UK. In coalition there was no prospect of change. Whilst pro-Europeans as well as those on the centre-left/left, such as Labour leader Jeremy Corbyn, viewed immigration and free movement of people as beneficial to the UK economy, concerns over the numbers of immigrants were apparent during the 2010 general election, as already discussed. Indeed, while membership of the EU had not been politically salient among ordinary voters (unlike the political class and journalists), immigration had become one of the top issues for voters. Prior to the 2005 election and Michael Howard's campaign, references to immigration had mostly been the preserve of the far right, particularly the National Front and later the British National Party (BNP). By 2010, however, immigration and EU membership began to come together thanks to UKIP, directly through their election campaigning and indirectly as the Conservative right endeavoured to squeeze out UKIP rather as the French centre-right sought to reduce the appeal of the French Front National; mainstream parties sought to retain control by taking political ground from increasingly successful Eurosceptic parties.

Attempts to reduce immigration could not include EU nationals as long as the UK remained in the EU. And while there were undoubted benefits from free movement – many of which were (and indeed continue to be) enjoyed by those individuals who had benefited from Erasmus schemes or exercised their rights as EU citizens to study, live, work or retire in other EU member states – there were significant flows of people in both directions. In practice, rather more EU nationals came to the UK than left to exercise their rights, leading to a significant net increase each year, although on a per capita basis more UK citizens exercised their rights of EU citizenship elsewhere in the EU. The movement of EU citizens, unlike numbers of third country nationals, could not be controlled by the UK. Yet already there were significant constraints on third country nationals, with student visas being very hard to come by, leading would-be students to apply to other English-speaking universities; this was a problem for one of the UK's largest service sector exports.

Vote Leave used immigration as a key vote-winning issue. Leading 'Brexiteer' Michael Gove, at the time a sitting Conservative Cabinet minister, even went so far as to criticise the Government's failure to curb immigration figures. Vote Leave also rather cleverly played to two separate audiences: overall they pressed the case to leave the EU in order to regain control of borders – and hence immigration numbers – and reduce net immigration volumes. This reflected a Conservative Party manifesto pledge that could not otherwise be delivered. Yet it was an issue that would resonate across parties, with former Labour supporters in the North of England voting Leave in significant numbers. Thus Gordon Brown's interlocutor Gillian Duffy had not been an aberration, as the Leave campaign had understood but mainstream parties had not. By contrast, in immigrant communities, notably areas with significant numbers of Commonwealth citizens (who, unlike EU nationals, had a vote in the referendum) or people of Commonwealth descent, Leave claimed that reducing the numbers of EU migrants in the UK would make it easier for residents to bring over family members. Thus, at public meetings there would often be a question by or about taxi drivers, stressing what was purported to be the 'racist' nature of EU free movement. What those advocating Leave neglected to admit was that the net numbers of third country nationals coming into the UK was around 189,000, i.e. more than the numbers from the EU and, crucially, considerably more than the tens of thousands the Conservatives were talking about. Thus, even in the event of a vote to leave there was unlikely to be a liberalisation of immigration rules for Commonwealth nationals or anyone else. Nonetheless, this message resonated with some voters and contributed to the success of Leave on 23 June.

Another former UK preference, namely enlargement, was now used against membership. A Vote Leave poster claimed that 'Turkey (population 76 million) is joining the EU'. Certainly enlargement had long been a UK preference and successive prime ministers had also made the case that Turkey should be allowed to join the Union. The logic of granting Turkey candidate status was one of conditionality; EU member states hoped that by giving Turkey the prospect of joining, they would also give it an incentive to reform in order to meet the standards outlined in the Copenhagen criteria. However, it was always clear to those involved in European decision-making that Turkey's prospect of membership was at best many years hence and in all probability might never occur, as Turkey seemed to move further from the human rights and democracy criteria required for membership, not to mention the fact that every member state has a veto over enlargement and regardless of UK preferences it seemed unlikely that Greece or Cyprus would consent to Turkish accession. Yet none of this stopped the Leavers, who persisted in making the claim, which they augmented with a map of Europe where the only countries named were Turkey's neighbours – Iran, Iraq and Syria. The intention was clearly to create concern among voters, not least with the additional overblown assertion that 76 million Turks would be coming once the country joined the EU. While the assertions of the Leavers that some countries, notably the Western Balkans and Turkey, would join in the near future and that they could do so by 2020 were always fanciful, the fact that David Cameron (like his UK predecessors) had advocated expansion to include Turkey could not be gainsaid, not least because of the negative signals it would have sent to Turkey. As with so much of the referendum, the arguments and the way in which they were articulated could be portrayed in very black-and-white terms, while the reality was inevitably far more nuanced.

The Leavers also tied three things together very effectively: fears of enlargement, the cost of EU membership and the British commitment to the NHS. Thus, in a single graphic they suggested that money was flowing out of the UK to would-be members such as Turkey, claiming that this amounted to £350 million per week and it represented money that could be spent on the NHS. This figure was contestable, at the very least, reflecting gross payments for which the UK would have been liable had there been no rebate, and neglecting the receipts that the UK has from the EU. The net figure was thus about half of the £350 million, but this did not matter in a referendum characterised by hysteria and hyperbole, where objective facts were hard to find. Attempts to correct the figure were simply met with the response, 'Well, it's still a lot of money'. That the rebate as not 'guaranteed' was used to reinforce their point. The Remainers failed to point out that while, yes, it was a lot of money, it represented only a tiny fraction of public expenditure, even compared with spending on the NHS. The Leavers' argument on this, as in so many areas, gained traction and the Remain campaign seemed incapable of refuting it. Indeed on many issues in the referendum, the efforts of experts, officials or mainstream politicians supporting the Remain side were shot down by mere assertions by naysayers on the Leave side. On one occasion the BBC's response to an open letter backing the Remain campaign that had been signed by more than 280 members of the creative industries was to say that Michael Dobbs, the author of the political thriller *House of Cards*, disagreed; none of the signatories of the letter were mentioned by name and the BBC, in its attempt to provide balance, effectively gave more publicity and credence to the Leave campaign than to Remain, whose initiative might reasonably have been expected to capture the headline. As on many occasions during the referendum, attempts by the Remainers to make a reasoned case were effectively denigrated by simple denials by the Leavers; the Remain camp seemed unable to retaliate against the Leavers' arguments.

The referendum was Remain's to lose. They had the benefits of: being the status quo option (normally seen as helpful in referendums, as voters are typically risk-averse); money and resources, including the machinery of government, at least until purdah kicked in (yet these were squandered); they had every global leader behind them, except, perhaps, Vladimir Putin, yet the interventions of these leaders, from Barack Obama down, were seen by many as an attempt to bully or coerce the UK. All of this played into the hands of the Leave campaign, which could argue convincingly that 'the Establishment is against us', which had traction even when those bemoaning the fact were themselves Cabinet Ministers or former Cabinet Ministers, member of the House of Lords or Oxbridge-educated Old Etonians. That they were able to do this might seem paradoxical but the difference was that the leaders of the Leave campaign had an emotive narrative that spoke to ordinary people, caught the imagination and, crucially, said 'We understand your concerns'. It mattered little where the leaders of Leave came from. What mattered was that, like Margaret Thatcher thirty years previously, they 'got' the average voter. By contrast, those campaigning to remain seemed out of touch. When Stephen Kinnock, son of former Labour leader and former EU Commissioner Neil (now Lord) Kinnock and former Minister for Europe Glenys (now Baroness) Kinnock, and husband of former Danish Prime Minister Helle Thorning-Schmidt, was able to say on the BBC's flagship *Today* programme that there were enough MPs and peers in favour of staying in the single market that in the event of a vote to leave they would be able to find a way around it, it became clear that many politicians were perhaps not listening to the voters; something that in large part helps explain how the UK had got into this situation in the first place.

Project Fear could not work a third time, lacking the skills of Lynton Crosby who was not persuaded of the merits of Remain, but was sufficiently loyal to the PM not to support the Leave campaign either, and with the media actively backing the other side. Where Better Together had enjoyed the support of most of the media and the Conservatives' Project Fear general election campaign of 2015 had enjoyed the support of the right-wing press, the majority of the print media were strongly opposed to membership of the EU, and had been waging war against it for many years. Even newspapers such as *The Times,* which finally came down for Remain, consistently produced strongly Eurosceptic articles. The 'Establishment' may have been against Leave, but the media and the money were not. And when the only poll that mattered – the referendum itself – came, the majority of those voting opted to leave.

The Outcome

The final result, in the early hours of 24 June 2016, came as a shock to campaigners on both sides. While the opinion polls and the mood in hustings and on doorsteps across the country had led some to anticipate a Leave vote as likely or at least possible, the results were met with a degree of incredulity in both camps. The Remain side had never been able to overcome either the complacency that had dogged the pro-EU side for years or the generally lacklustre campaign. Yet even in the middle of the count, Ryan Coetzee was claiming a narrow victory (Oliver 2016). Michael Gove's wife, the journalist Sarah Vine (Vine 2016), wrote the following week that she had told him, 'You were only supposed to blow the bloody doors off.' Certainly both Gove and fellow Leave campaigner Boris Johnson appeared shocked when they finally gave a press conference at 11am on 24 June. Neither side had planned for a vote to Leave. The Leavers had argued it was for the Government to do so; they could not, as they were just an insurgent group, pressing for a vote to leave but expecting/requiring others to effect the departure. Meanwhile, one reason why the Government had been so reluctant to provide an objective analysis of what Leave would look like became clear: it had not done the work either, the Treasury's 'scenarios' notwithstanding. There was no Plan B. A Prime Minister who was determined to offer the people a choice on whether to stay in the EU had not allowed even preliminary plans for the alternative outcome to be devised. The people had voted to Leave, but quite how the UK would leave the EU and what their future relations might look like was no clearer on 24 June than before the referendum. The Vote to Leave was just the beginning of a whole new European journey for the UK and the destination remained unknown.

Note

1 For fuller analyses of the legislation on the referendum and the nature of parliamentary engagement, see Smith 2016 and Smith forthcoming.

7   Where do we Go from Here?

'Brexit means Brexit' (Reprise)

As soon as the result of the 2016 referendum was known, Theresa May, at that time still Home Secretary and officially a Remainer, stated that she accepted the outcome and coined the line that would become her catchphrase in the subsequent weeks and months: 'Brexit means Brexit'. It was a firm, confident statement, but one that was meaningless tautology. Yet it highlighted the problem facing the UK in the wake of the referendum: if the implications of 'Leave' had not been clarified by its advocates during the referendum, those who had advocated 'Remain' certainly had no blueprint for leaving. May was asserting that she had accepted the result of the referendum and would not seek to overturn it – as many Remainers initially hoped to do.[1] But what does leaving the EU really mean?

'We aren't leaving "Europe". We love Europe. We take our holidays there. It's the EU we hate.' So argued the Leavers during the referendum campaign and into the summer of 2016. Of course they were correct. The vote to leave the EU clearly did not alter the fundamental principles of geography: the UK was and remains a European country. Nor did the vote immediately alter the UK's relationship with the EU. While many voters spoke of 'having left the EU' in the aftermath of the referendum, moves to depart were set to take years and would not commence until Article 50 of the Treaty on European Union was triggered. In order to leave the EU, the UK is required to trigger Article 50, which provides the mechanism for a member state to withdraw under the Lisbon Treaty provisions. Once triggered, there is a two-year timeframe for negotiations, after which the withdrawing state would be out of the EU without a deal of any sort if one had not been reached by then. In addition, the UK needs to repeal the European Communities Act 1972, which was the source of contention for so many

Eurosceptics over the years. However, there is far more at stake in actually leaving the European Union than simply invoking Article 50 and repealing the 1972 Act. During more than four decades of membership, the sheer weight of EU legislation grew enormously, at times at the behest of the UK and generally with its agreement. Some of that legislation was incorporated into UK domestic law and can thus remain in force after the UK formally leaves the EU. Other legislation which has 'direct effect' while the UK remains a member of the EU would in practical terms need to be incorporated into UK law or otherwise be replaced. This could be done by a single portmanteau bill, effectively confirming that all EU legislation in place at the time of withdrawal would remain on the statute book until amended or repealed. Thus, in October 2016 the Prime Minister promised that a Great Repeal Bill, the title redolent of major, usually positive, constitutional reforms of the past, would be brought forward in the 2017–18 session of Parliament. Whether, of course, all Leavers understood the possibility of EU law being enshrined into UK law in this way is unknown, but it seems unlikely that those seeking to reduce regulation would have anticipated this route to regaining control.

Article 50 and the proposed Great Repeal Act are in many ways the easy parts of withdrawal. In the event of 'hard Brexit', taken to mean leaving the EU without seeking any form of co-operation beyond a trading relationship, entirely outside the single market and the customs union, the UK would be free to negotiate new trading relations with third countries as soon as it has withdrawn from the EU. Yet Article 50 also states that the withdrawal agreement should take into consideration the withdrawing state's future relationship with the EU. That would prove a much bigger hurdle for the UK as it looked beyond the vote to leave the EU and assessed where and how its interests would best be served. Leaving the EU might prove the easiest part of the job, though the aftermath of the referendum highlighted just how hard this process could be as legal challenges swiftly emerged.

Who Can File for Divorce?

The timing and formality of the triggering of Article 50 proved a source of major political and legal controversy in the weeks and months after the vote to leave. Some of the UK's 27 EU partners – as well as Commission President Juncker – were keen for the UK to invoke the 'divorce clause' immediately, arguing that the vote was clear, the UK was on its way out of the EU and it should not delay matters further. Angela Merkel, ever the pragmatist, took the view that the UK should be given some time before starting the two-year process, aware that its Government needed time to begin to prepare its proposals for the sort of relationship it would ideally desire after withdrawal. Given the absence of any Plan B by the Government or the Leave campaign, some breathing space was essential.

Since the Conservative Party had agreed to be bound by the outcome of the referendum, the logical response to the outcome of the referendum was to trigger Article 50 – the only legal route to depart from the EU. Simply to repeal the European Communities Act 1972, as some Leavers had proposed, would put the UK in breach of not just EU law – arguably a moot point, given the vote to leave – but also international law. Not only could that course of action invoke legal challenges – ironically, given Vote Leave's 'take back control' mantra was in part a reaction against the role of courts – it could also antagonise the other 27 member states and the EU institutions, thereby rendering them less likely to agree a favourable ongoing relationship. For Theresa May, the cool-headed Remainer turned 'Brexiteer', the course of action was straightforward: she would trigger Article 50 at such time as her Government was sufficiently prepared; in the autumn of 2016 she said she intended to launch the process by the end of March 2017.

Who, exactly, has the right to invoke Article 50? Prior to the referendum, David Cameron indicated that he would trigger Article 50 within days of a vote to the leave the EU. In the event he resigned immediately and left the job to his successor. The incoming PM accepted the advice of government lawyers that she could trigger Article 50 using prerogative powers, cutting Westminster out of the process. May was clear that she had the right to act under Royal Prerogative – the same powers that traditionally allow Prime Ministers to take the country to war without a parliamentary vote. Yet even in the context of the decision to go to war, the issue of Royal Prerogative has been challenged in recent years (Gray and Lomas 2014). In the case of EU withdrawal, the decision to hold the referendum and the Government's commitment to be bound by it led some to believe that **politically** the decision had been made by the voters, and further parliamentary approval was not needed to invoke Article 50 even if it would be required at later stages of the withdrawal process.

There was a logic to May's position. The UK may pride itself on having the 'mother of parliaments', but the decision to hold an 'in/out' referendum that was translated into law in the European Union Referendum Act 2015 essentially returned sovereign powers to the people. The referendum of 23 June 2016 was subsequent to the general election that had elected the 650 members of the UK Parliament, a clear majority of whom wished the country to remain in the EU. Any parliamentary vote attempting to overturn the result of the referendum would thus have been seen as a way to try to circumvent the will of the people. Such arguments may appear to be a travesty of representative democracy but they are the logical corollary of holding the referendum in the first place. If MPs had not wanted the citizens to make this momentous decision, they should not have offered the referendum in the first place.

Of course, many Remainers would vehemently argue that the UK's famously uncodified constitution means that this referendum could not bind parliament. Legally, they are undoubtedly correct. But politically it is hard to see how MPs and peers who voted through the legislation permitting the referendum to occur could turn round and say after the fact, 'We don't accept the result; it wasn't binding.' At no point did the then Prime Minister or representatives of the Government or Opposition say it would not be binding; indeed, Cameron was explicit that the result would be respected. Any attempt to try to prevent Brexit through a parliamentary vote would thus be politically very dangerous and would certainly vindicate the criticisms of Leavers about the EU's unwillingness to accept the verdict of disaffected voters in repeated referendums. Since the only legal way to leave the EU is through the Article 50 process, then the vote to leave could be construed as a mandate to trigger it.

This view was not held by a series of litigants who sought to prevent the PM from using prerogative powers to invoke Article 50. The crowd-funded People's Challenge 'told the court they are arguing the UK's constitutional arrangements mean that only Parliament can lawfully "decide" to leave the EU for the purposes of article 50 TEU; and that [David Davis] may only "notify" such a decision to the European Council under Article 50(2) TEU once he has been properly authorised to do so by an act of parliament' (Fenton 2016). Regardless of the technical issues of prerogative power, a parliamentary vote seemed politically desirable – if the citizens had voted to 'take back control' of their laws, then involving parliament was the obvious way to do so. A votable motion would allow Parliament to be fully engaged as the Government says its wishes it to be, and help set the terms of the negotiations to depart, but would not serve as a block to triggering Article 50. However, the Government was reluctant to concede any parliamentary involvement beyond debates without votes and a promise of being 'engaged', and the legal challenges reached the courts.

The High Court rejected the Government's case. In their judgement *R (Miller) v Secretary of State for Exiting the European Union*, given on 3 November 2016, the Divisional Court ruled that the Royal Prerogative did not apply in the case of triggering Article 50 (Miller 2016). Primary legislation would be required before Article 50 could be triggered. The Government immediately announced that it would appeal. For the Government and many furious Leavers who castigated the judges' decision, 'taking back control' seemed to mean not returning power to Westminster, but to No. 10. Courts, the bane of many Leavers, became the new ground for contestation over potential Brexit, with the ironic twist that the ultimate court of appeal could be the Court of Justice of the EU.

But it was not only Westminster that needed to have its say. The devolved parliaments, assemblies and governments in Scotland, Wales and Northern Ireland all clamoured – and had the right – to be heard. Yet their constitutional rights in the context of Brexit were as obscure as those of Westminster. Theresa May visited the Scottish First Minister Nicola Sturgeon two days after becoming PM, acknowledging the significance of Scotland and Sturgeon's desire to press for a second independence referendum, for which she announced preliminary plans on the morning of 24 June. There appeared no way that Scotland, Northern Ireland or Gibraltar, all of which had supported staying in the EU, could overturn the results for themselves. Yet, given the alacrity with which lawyers representing Remainers launched actions to try to prevent or delay triggering Article 50, similar actions on behalf of these populations could not be ruled out. The constitutional implications of the decision to hold the referendum and its outcome on the UK – particularly regarding Northern Ireland and relations with the Republic – had not been thought through, and would be among the many issues to be resolved before the UK finally left the EU.

When to Leave?

Just as Cameron's decision to set a date by which the referendum must be held limited his ability to negotiate the best deal for the UK and hampered the Remain campaign's ability to win the referendum, so the withdrawal negotiations would be affected by timing. While the UK could technically delay invoking Article 50 indefinitely, it came under some pressure from fellow member states to get on with it, after a reasonable period of preparation. To do otherwise would merely create additional uncertainty in the other 27 member states and the UK, which would be bad for business and bad for individual citizens and their families. The negotiations would be affected by various timetables, with the domestic perhaps less significant than those of the EU and the other member states. The Fixed-term Parliaments Act 2011 meant the PM had until May 2020 to 'deliver Brexit' before the next general election. The French and German elections, which Cameron had sought to avoid during his renegotiation, would mean that neither country would be able to devote much attention to Brexit negotiations before late 2017. Merkel's departure from the European stage, whether forced or voluntary, would fundamentally alter the negotiations, partly because of personal relations and her efforts to keep the UK in the EU, and partly because of her experience and role as a senior statesman in Europe. The departure of François Hollande would be less of a challenge for the UK, unless the (almost) unthinkable occurred in the form of Marine Le Pen becoming President, but nevertheless the prospect of electoral upheaval elsewhere in the EU would affect negotiations.

On the EU agenda, the new budgetary and institutional cycles would be affected by, and would affect, the UK's prospective departure. Revision of the Union's budget in the form of a review of the MFF was due and the EU would need to be able to model the new arrangements without a major contributor, the UK – unless, of course, the UK adopted a Norwegian-style arrangement as a member of the European Economic Area or as part of a sui generis deal, which would include paying into the EU budget – not anticipated by most Leavers, who hoped to stem monies flowing 'to Brussels', but not excluded in Theresa May's calls for a 'bespoke' deal. While the precise details could be finalised at a later date, some indication of where the UK was going would assist those involved in budgetary preparations. EP elections will be held in mid-2019 and thereafter the new Commission, European Council President and the High Representative of the Union for Foreign Affairs and Security Policy would be appointed. The logical time for the UK to leave would be early 2019, neatly coinciding with the end of the 2014–19 mandate. The UK could not be compelled to do so, but that approach would be institutionally neat.

What Sort of Brexit under Theresa May?

Theresa May's 'Brexit means Brexit' statement sounded clear and decisive when she first uttered it in July 2016, but it was ultimately tautological and without content. Some battle lines did begin to emerge in the autumn of 2016, yet all options seemed fraught with difficulty in a Conservative Party that remained divided over the best approach to take. Almost all coalesced around the idea that the vote meant the UK was leaving the EU, but they did not agree what sort of future relationship would be desirable. Staying in a single market would create untold difficulties for hardline Eurosceptics who sought complete withdrawal from the Union including from the single market, an end to budgetary contributions and free movement of people. Yet this was precisely what many in Labour and the Liberal Democrats – as well as pro-EU Conservatives – were calling for. To assist the economy, they believed, membership of – not just access to – the single market is crucial. What matters are not just tariffs but non-tariff barriers to trade (which the single market served to eliminate over the course of nearly thirty years) and, crucially, free movement of people.

However, the focus on the UK's demands from the EU as it prepared to leave the Union misses a crucial, and much neglected, aspect of Article 50. The provision is not about negotiation, in the way that David Cameron undertook to renegotiate the UK's terms of membership. It is asymmetric in that the 27 remaining partners agree the deal and the withdrawing state, as the *demandeur*, gets to take it or leave it. Article 50 is as yet untested, and it is theoretically possible that the rest of the EU will be generous and willing to rethink the deal on offer if it does not seem satisfactory to the UK. Yet they have all the bargaining chips; the UK is not in a strong position. And, as always in EU affairs, there is the need for the leaders of the 27 partner states to think both of the European interest and their own national interests and domestic constituencies. It is not only David Cameron, Theresa May and British politicians who have such constraints to consider. The UK will perhaps come to realise all of these issues too late. After all, each of the 27 continuing members has a veto over the deal offered to the withdrawing state, and depending on the type of ongoing relationship sought, each national parliament in the 27, plus some sub-national parliaments, may also have a vote, and a veto.

Nonetheless it is important for the withdrawing state to have some sense of what it hopes to achieve through withdrawing, to set the terms for what life outside the EU means. When Labour's Roger Liddle wondered ahead of the referendum what 'Leave' would look like, there were few answers. The most honest response came from UKIP MEP (and very briefly leader), Diane James, who said in answer to one question on the BBC's *Question Time* programme just a few weeks before the referendum: 'We just don't know.' It was perhaps the most honest, yet also the most troubling response coming from either proponents of Leave or Remainers. There was no Plan B.

That it was for Leavers to define what leave meant would be a constant refrain during the referendum itself: the Prime Minister, Government and the official Remain campaign all called on the Leave campaign to outline their vision of what leaving would mean. The

Leavers appeared rather aghast that they should be asked to provide answers to this question, several key figures suggesting it would be for the PM to sort out in the event of a Leave vote. The Leavers did not have a single coherent vision of what the alternative to membership should be. Some argued that the UK could simply default to World Trade Organization terms of trade, a position that seemed to be clear and offered the possibility of reducing immigration or ending free movement from the EU in line with the claims of 'Vote Leave' during the referendum, although the financial implications of such a move were unclear and WTO membership would require agreement from all 164 existing members as the UK's membership is as part of the EU. Others seemed to support a relationship akin to that of Norway, a member of the EEA.

Theresa May appointed not one but three ministers to have responsibility for Brexit – David Davis, a former Minister of State for Europe (under Major, at the time of the BSE crisis) as Secretary of State for Exiting the European Union; Liam Fox as Secretary of State for International Trade; and Boris Johnson as Foreign Secretary. All three had campaigned to leave the EU, and it seemed that May had appointed them on the principle 'You broke it; you fix it'. The three men had somewhat differing views over the relationship they sought with the EU – Johnson, for example, who had only been a last-minute convert to the Brexit cause, talked at one stage of remaining within the single market, while Fox was seen to favour a cleaner break. Quite the direction the Government would take took months to emerge as May shot down her ministers almost as soon as they aired their views, with her office repeatedly referring to Ministers speaking 'personally'.

Fox's role was particularly tricky. The Leave campaign had made a strong case for global trade, arguing that the EU was a declining market which would in any case wish to keep trading with the UK, but that there were far greater opportunities to trade if only the UK could escape the EU. However, while Fox and his team made preliminary approaches regarding the possibility of trade agreements he was rapidly rebuffed by the European Commission, which reminded him that trade is an exclusive EU competence; the Commission negotiates trade deals on behalf of the EU, and any attempt by a member state (even one that was leaving the EU) to undertake such negotiations would be found in breach of the treaties and could result in a fine. While such a course of action might seem draconian, the fact that the Commission raised the threat highlighted how little the Government would be able to achieve prior to leaving the EU, and indeed how little the UK seemed to understand the EU game after more than forty years of membership. Meanwhile Boris Johnson's FCO was a diminished entity following years of cuts, compounded by the fact that the most important European affairs were now part of Davis's new Department, just at a time when the FCO needed more resources, not fewer, in order to rebuild the bilateral embassies in EU capitals, which had seen their role diminish since the UK joined the EU, as so much business was done directly.

The key choice facing the UK was whether to try to remain part of the single market for which it had pushed so hard under Margaret Thatcher and which was seen by Cameron as crucial to the UK, forming part of the 2015 general election manifesto and of his renegotiation. Many of those who had campaigned to remain in the EU believed that the best alternative would be for the UK to remain as closely tied to the EU as possible, essentially meaning ongoing membership of the single market, with the four freedoms that this entailed. Here there was a tension – a key part of the single market is free movement of people to which other member states were wedded, especially the four Visegrad (V4) countries (Poland, Hungary, Slovakia and the Czech Republic), which had been actively courted by the UK under Tony Blair and whose citizens had made extensive use of their free movement rights. Each of them would have a veto over the UK's withdrawal deal. For the V4 countries, retaining free movement was crucial. For all member states the link was unbreakable – there would be no membership of the single market without free movement of people, they asserted, as did European business leaders. That this freedom went far beyond that envisaged in the founding Treaty of Rome, which referred only to free movement of 'labour' went unexplored, but it was a shift that had contributed to the UK's frustration with the EU. An agreement to revert to the position might have been acceptable to the UK but would it/could it be accepted by the other 27 member states? This was the sort of issue that should have been considered before the referendum, even if the Government had not wished either voters or other member states to know it was contemplating the possibly of a vote to leave.

The knock-on effects of free movement would be seen in the wake of the vote to Leave, in the somewhat surreal form of senior members of the Leave campaign making impassioned demands for the Government to confirm the rights of EU nationals already resident in the UK (see Hansard for various questions and debates in July 2016). The hard realities of the case they had made for curbing free movement seemed to have come home to Leavers who suddenly realised that it would create massive uncertainties for individuals and their families, which in turn would create problems for businesses, including crucial sectors ranging from finance to fruit-picking and – most poignantly given its central role in the Leave campaign's narrative – the NHS. There was broad, cross-party support for such calls, with initially only Theresa May as Home Secretary actively disagreeing. By October 2016 May's line had been adopted by the Secretary of State for International Trade, Liam Fox, who argued that these people would be pawns in a complex Brexit game, possibly used to secure the rights of UK citizens living or working elsewhere in the EU.

The majority of Leavers, who were not racist, were as shaken as those who had favoured remaining by the fact that a minority of people had taken the Leave vote as an excuse to perpetrate hate crimes, particularly against Poles. While Leavers were keen to distance themselves from the taint of racism, one saying that 'racism was wholly incidental to the Leave campaign' (source: private communication with a Leave MP, August 2016) it was clear in the immediate aftermath of the referendum that many EU nationals had begun to feel unwelcome in the UK and had begun to question whether they had a long-term future there, even before Article 50 was triggered. The election of Theresa May as PM and her appointment of former Foreign Secretary Philip Hammond as Chancellor of the Exchequer ensured that the hard-line position regarding the need to consider the position of EU nationals in light of decisions taken on the rights of UK nationals by other member states left these individuals in limbo, with a sense that they were negotiating pawns; a position reinforced by Fox's statement. That the PM clearly understood that it was important not to show one's negotiating hand too soon further reinforced a sense that this was a very instrumental approach that did little to help community cohesion or relations with other member states.

Nothing Changes until the Day the UK leaves the EU ... or Does it?

When pressed about the rights of EU nationals resident in the UK, ministers' default response in the weeks after the referendum was simply that 'Nothing changes until we leave'. They gradually nuanced their response to say that they hoped to be able to guarantee these rights, the only exception being if other EU states did not guarantee the rights of UK nationals resident in their countries – a scenario that they could not envisage, or so they said. What they did not acknowledge was that the situation for EU nationals changed as soon as the referendum outcome was announced. For some this was tangible in the form of racist calls to 'go home', and worse, as some people turned to hate crimes, using the immigration dimension of the Leave campaign as justification, despite the widespread repudiation of these actions by all mainstream politicians, whichever side of the Brexit debate they had supported. For others there was a more intangible sense of feeling less welcome on 24 June than they had previously, coupled with a concern that no-one could tell them what their position would be the day after the UK left the EU. 'Nothing changes', ministers kept asserting. But everything had changed. Uncertainly had come into the lives of many EU nationals who began to ponder whether they should not look to move jobs and homes to relocate themselves and their families to another EU member state.

Other things changed too. The UK's Jonathan Hill resigned from his post as European Commissioner for Financial Stability, Financial Services and Capital Markets Union just days after the referendum, even though the UK is entitled to representation in all the EU institutions until the day it leaves. While Hill was replaced as British European Commissioner by seasoned diplomat Julian King, the prized financial services portfolio was rapidly passed on to the Latvian Commissioner and King was given a new security portfolio. This may have been appropriate, given the UK's apparent interest in retaining security links with the EU once it had left, but it was nonetheless an early sign that the UK's influence within the EU was waning even before Article 50 was triggered. When it was announced that the UK would not be holding the six-monthly rotating presidency in the second half of 2017, the prospect of separation became even more real.

Moreover, while the withdrawing state can indicate the type of ongoing relationship it wishes to have with the remaining EU, the process is asymmetric: when the EU is agreeing its position the withdrawing country has no seat at the table. Moves towards meetings of the 'EU-27' (i.e. the EU-28 minus the UK) began even before the UK had triggered Article 50. The Bratislava meeting of the Heads of State and Government of the EU-27, held on 16 September 2016, highlighted some of the serious challenges and divisions facing the EU in its eighth decade: its members may agree on the problems they face but not on the ways to resolve them. The outcome of the first meeting of the 27 remaining states, focusing on life in the EU beyond Brexit, saw a renewal of the Franco-German bonds and a commitment to further integration; two scenarios which would not have occurred without the catalyst of Brexit, with further integration being anathema to British Eurosceptics, while Franco-German relations had been weakening for years until this new impetus forced them together again. As a member of the EU the UK has a seat at the table and can block undesirable treaty changes: outside the Union it will not be able to do so, as Bratislava already foreshadowed. Yet the outcome for the EU itself is uncertain, as Juncker noted in September 2016: 'Never before have I seen such little common ground between our member states, so few areas where they agree to work together' (quoted in Waterfield 2016). The UK would be at the mercy of 27 countries which will find it difficult to agree among themselves and which have quite varied interests in the EU and their ongoing relationship with the UK. By focusing almost exclusively on their own demands and wishes, Britons – Brexiteers and Remainers alike – tend to neglect the importance of the European-level negotiations. The UK can make its views clear, but ultimately decision-making power rests with the EU-27. The process of leaving and finding a new *modus vivendi* could be very protracted indeed.

Coming Full Circle

The perennial themes of sovereignty, free trade and the financial cost of membership which had kept the UK out of the European Communities in the early years, had gone on to play a key role in accession debates, and the renegotiation and referendum processes of the 1970s, and had driven an-ever deepening Euroscepticism, augmented by the new-found objections to the results of deliberate decisions by the Blair Government, which agreed to both a rapid expansion of the EU without restrictions on free movement and to a reduction of the UK's budgetary rebate, all affected the 2016 referendum campaigns and their outcomes. Moreover, the same issues would also set the scene for the subsequent wrangles over the future relationship that the UK should have with the rest of the EU after its eventual departure. Here, the tensions of Brexit demands and the commitment of some Brexiteers and most Remainers became starkly clear. To 'square the circle' of access to the single market, cutting or at least reducing the cost of membership, curbing free movement and regaining sovereignty is a nigh on impossible task. It is possible, of course, for the UK to have 'access' to the single market; that is true for any country wishing to trade with the EU regardless of any deal it strikes with the Union. However, what appears most commonly to be understood by 'access' is in fact 'membership', which is what is needed if the benefits of the market – including the removal not just of tariffs but, more importantly, of non-tariff barriers – are to be secured. Yet it is inconceivable that the future EU-27 would allow the UK more favourable terms than they themselves enjoy. Membership of the single market short of EU membership requires obedience to EU rules (but without a seat at the table), as well as paying into the EU budget, not to mention acceptance of EU rules on the free movement of people – a perennial difficulty for the UK.

So formally regaining sovereignty comes at a high price – and one that almost certainly would not be acceptable to many of those who advocate Brexit so passionately, nor to those voters who believed that Brexit would provide more money to the NHS and reduce the numbers of immigrants. Some Leavers (such as Bernard Jenkin) argue there is no difference between 'hard Brexit' and 'soft Brexit' – the latter being understood as an ongoing relationship with the EU that falls short of membership, but could include membership of the single market and the associated rights and responsibilities – and to an extent they are right, as the issue is really the relationship that comes after the UK leaves the European Union. 'Hard Brexit' would presumably satisfy those who wish to reclaim sovereignty and end payments to Brussels, but the ultimate costs to the UK economy are unknown territory. Indeed the Treasury's pre-referendum scenarios, decried as part of Project Fear by the Leavers at the time, might prove their worth in the event that the future relationship does not include a clearly defined trade agreement post-Brexit. It seemed that in voting to leave the EU the UK had little sense of what the future would hold: its destination was fundamentally unclear, just as it had been in the 1970s.

David Cameron set the timetable that culminated with the Brexit vote of 2016. From then on, the UK's future relationship with Europe would increasingly depend rather on the whims and timings of the rest of the EU more than perhaps anyone in the UK, be they Remainer or Leaver, had ever really thought through before the whole 'reform, renegotiation and referendum' mantra was introduced. The UK may have voted to leave the EU but that was merely the start of the long and rocky journey out of the Union. In 2017 the UK's European future remained, paradoxically, as uncertain as it had appeared 45 years earlier when Shonfield gave his 1972 Reith Lectures. The UK was still on a 'journey to an unknown destination'.

Note

1 A petition to introduce various thresholds into the referendum retrospectively, which would have effectively nullified the outcome, rapidly secured over four million signatures as desperate Remainers sought a way out of the unwelcome referendum result. Cities like London and Cambridge immediately began pro-EU campaigns such as London Stays (later amalgamated into Stand Together). Yet by the time the petition was debated in Westminster Hall on 5 September 2016, the heat seemed to have gone out of the campaign to overturn the referendum. The focus had shifted to enabling voters to have a say on whatever withdrawal package was ultimately negotiated.

8 Postscript

In January 2017 certain aspects of the UK's moves towards the European departure lounge became clear. Six months after taking office Prime Minister Theresa May finally outlined her objectives for the negotiations in a keynote address at Lancaster House (May 2017). She made clear that she had understood the tension between membership of the single market and curbing free movement of people. In a blow for those hoping for a 'soft Brexit' she announced that the UK would not be seeking ongoing membership of the single market. Nor would membership of the Customs Union necessarily be on the cards since that would curtail the UK's hopes of a forging new free trade deals. While the announcement demonstrated a degree of understanding of the concerns of the other 27 EU member states who were anxious that by leaving the EU the UK should not enjoy better terms than the ongoing members, May's announcement was not welcome to those who hoped to minimise the impact of leaving the EU by remaining as close as possible to the EU. Their views may have been disregarded had May been able to use the royal prerogative to trigger Article 50 as she had hoped. However, the Supreme Court's majority judgement dismissing the Government's appeal against the High Court's ruling in Miller ensured that the Government would have to pass primary legislation (Supreme Court 2017). While most Conservatives and many Labour MPs said they would not vote against Article 50, indeed Jeremy Corbyn stated that Labour MPs would not block Article 50, the need for legislation will provide a parliamentary forum for many issues surrounding the UK's future relations with the EU to be rehearsed. If citizens had voted to 'take back control', the Courts had ensured that it would be parliament and not the executive that would exercise that control.

Julie Smith/24 January 2017

References

Agence Europe (1991) 'Press Conference held by European Commission President Jacques Delors and European Council President Ruud Lubbers after the Intergovernmental Conference in Maastricht', 12 December, extracts reprinted in A. G. Harryvan and J. van der Harst, eds, *Documents on European Union* (Houndmills and London: Macmillan Press Ltd, 1997), pp. 267–271.

Baker, David, Andrew Gamble and Steve Ludlam (1993) 'Whips or Scorpions? The Maastricht Vote and the Conservative Party', *Parliamentary Affairs*, Vol. 46, No. 2, pp. 151–166.

Baker, David, Andrew Gamble and Steve Ludlam (1994) 'The Parliamentary Siege of Maastricht 1993: Conservative Divisions and British Ratification', *Parliamentary Affairs*, Vol. 47, No. 1, pp. 37–59.

BBC News website (2012) 'EU budget vote: Rebel MPs defeat government over spending cut call', 31 October, available at: http://www.bbc.co.uk/news/uk-politics-20157063, accessed on 17 September 2016.

Blair, Tony (2010) *A Journey* (London: Hutchinson).

Brugmans, Hendrik (1970) 'Foreword' to Schelto Patijn, ed., *Landmarks in European Unity – 22 Texts on European Integration* (Leiden: A.W. Sijthoff), cited in Julie Smith (1999) *Europe's Elected Parliament* (Sheffield: Sheffield Academic Press), p. 34.

Butler, David and Uwe Kitzinger (1996) *The 1975 Referendum* (Basingstoke: Palgrave Macmillan, 2nd edition) .

Cameron, David (2013) EU Speech at Bloomberg, 23 January, available at: www.gov.uk/government/speeches/eu-speech-at-bloomberg, accessed on 24 September 2016.

Cameron, David (2014) 'David Cameron's immigration speech: full text', *The Spectator*, available at http://blogs.spectator.co.uk/2014/11/david-camerons-immigration-speech-full-text/, accessed on 25 September 2016.

Cameron, David (2015) 'A New Settlement for the United Kingdom in a Reformed European Union', Letter to European Council President Donald Tusk, 10 November.

Cash, Sir William [Bill] (2014) Interview with the author, 8 September 2014.

References

Cash, William (2016) 'The Deep History of Brexit', *The Sunday Times Magazine*, 7 August, pp. 22–27.

Churchill, Winston S. (1946) 'The Tragedy of Europe' in Brent F. Nelsen and Alexander C.-G. Stubb, eds, *The European Union – Readings on the Theory and Practice of European Integration* (Boulder, CO: Lynne Rienner Publishers, Inc, 1994) pp. 5–9.

Clegg, Nick (2016) *Politics Between the Extremes* (London: Bodley Head).

Cockfield, Lord [Arthur] (1994) *The European Union – Creating the Single Market* (Chichester: Chancery Law Ltd).

Conservative Party (2014) *Conservative Party European Election Manifesto 2014*.

Conservative Party (2015) *Strong Leadership, A Clear Economic Plan, A Brighter, More Secure Future: The Conservative Party Manifesto 2015*.

Cook, Robin (2003) *The Point of Departure* (London: Simon and Schuster).

Deighton, Anne (ed.) (1995) *Building Postwar Europe – National Decision-Makers and European Institutions 1948–63* (Basingstoke: Macmillan Press Ltd).

Daily Express (2011) Petition homepage, available at: http://www.express.co.uk/web/referendum, accessed on 17 September 2016.

De Gaulle, Charles (1963) 'Press statement by French president Charles de Gaulle', reprinted in Harryvan and van der Harst, op. cit., pp. 132–136. [Original printed in Charles de Gaulle, *Discours et Messages. Pour l'effort Août 1962 – Décembre 1965* (Paris: Librairie Plon, 1970), pp. 66–70.]

De Gaulle, Charles (1967) 'Extract from press statement by French President Charles de Gaulle' in Harryvan and van der Harst, op. cit., pp. 156–159.

Elliott, Francis (2016) 'Cameron said no to personal attacks on leading Brexiteers', *The Times*, 24 September, available at: www.thetimes.co.uk/article/cameron-said-no-to-personal-attacks-on-leading-brexiteers-wv2pcgdwr, accessed on 3 December 2016.

Evening Standard (2014) 'Lords kill off EU referendum bill', 31 January, available at: www.standard.co.uk/panewsfeeds/lords-kill-off-eu-referendum-bill-9099882.html, accessed on 17 September 2016.

Fenton, Siobhan (2016) 'Government forced to reveal "secret arguments" for triggering Article 50 ahead of anti-Brexit legal challenge', *The Independent*, 28 September, available at: www.independent.co.uk/news/uk/politics/brexit-peoples-challenge-legal-high-court-block-article-50-referendum-a7335201.html, accessed on 29 September 2016.

Foreign and Commonwealth Office (1982) 'Britain in the European Community – The Budget Problem', extracts reprinted in T. Salmon and Sir W. Nicol, eds, *Building European Union – A documentary history and analysis* (Manchester: Manchester University Press, 1997) pp. 182–189.

Forster, Anthony (1999) *Britain and the Maastricht Negotiations* (Basingstoke: Macmillan Press Ltd).

Forster, Anthony (2002) *Euroscepticism in Contemporary British Politics – Opposition to Europe in the British Conservative and Labour Parties since 1945* (London and New York: Routledge).

Forsyth, Michael [Lord] (2009) Speech at dinner to celebrate thirtieth anniversary of Conservative election victory of 1979, available at: http://conservative home.blogs.com/files/forsyth-thatcher-speech.pdf, last accessed 2 December 2016.

Forsyth, Michael [Lord] (2013) 'Margaret Thatcher: She never stopped serving her country', *The Daily Telegraph*, 9 April, www.telegraph.co.uk/news/politics/margaret-thatcher/8523855/Margaret-Thatcher-She-never-stopped-serving-her-country.html, accessed on 6 August 2016.

Forsyth, Michael [Lord] (2016) Interview with author, House of Lords, 13 April.

George, Stephen (1991) *Britain and European Integration since 1945* (Oxford: Blackwell Publishers).

George, Stephen (1998) *An Awkward Partner: Britain in the European Community* (Oxford: Oxford University Press, 3rd edition).

Giscard d'Estaing, Valéry (2007) 'The EU Treaty is the same as the Constitution', *The Independent*, 30 October, available at: www.independent.co.uk/voices/commentators/valeacutery-giscard-destaing-the-eu-treaty-is-the-same-as-the-constitution-398286.html, accessed on 2 November 2016.

Gordon, Tom (2016) 'Better Together "absolutely appalling" says Tory grandee Michael Forsyth', *Herald Scotland*, 18 September, available at: www.heraldscotland.com/news/14749806.Better_Together__quot_absolutely_appalling_quot___says_Tory_grandee_Michael_Forsyth/, accessed on 28 September 2016.

Gray, James and Mark Lomas (2014) *Who Takes Britain to War?* (Stroud: The History Press).

Hannan, Daniel (2016) *Why Vote Leave* (London: Head of Zeus).

Harper, John (1996) 'In Their Own Image – The Americans and the Question of European Unity, 1943–1954', in Martyn Bond, Julie Smith and William Wallace, eds, *Eminent Europeans* (London: Greycoat Press), pp. 62–84.

Heath, Edward (1998) *The Course of My Life* (London: Hodder and Stoughton).

HM Government (2010) *The Coalition: our programme for government.*

HM Government (2016) *The best of both worlds: the United Kingdom's special status in a reformed European Union* (London: FCO).

House of Commons Information Office (1999) *HC Fact Sheet No. 68: General Election Results, 1 May 1997*, available at: www.parliament.uk/documents/commons-information-office/m15.pdf, accessed on 3 December 2016.

Jenkin, Bernard (2016) 'There is no such thing as hard or soft Brexit', *Financial Times*, 31 July, available at: www.ft.com/cms/s/0/f7764e16-5635-11e6-9f70-badea1b336d4.html#axzz4FvvTkN9d, accessed 2 August 2016.

Johnson, Simon (2016) 'Michael Forsyth: SNP dream of Scottish independence in Europe is a "cruel lie"', *The Daily Telegraph*, 12 May, available at: www.telegraph.co.uk/news/2016/05/12/michael-forsyth-snp-dream-of-scottish-independence-in-europe-is/, accessed on 3 December 2016.

Lamont, Norman (2016) Interview with the author, 5 May.

References

Lawson, Dominic (1990) 'Saying the Unsayable about the Germans', *The Spectator*, 14 July.

Lawson, Nigel (2016) Interview with the author, 14 July.

May, Theresa (2017) Speech on the government's negotiating objectives for exiting the EU given at Lancaster House on 17 January 2017, available at https://www.gov.uk/government/speeches/the-governments-negotiating-objectives-for-exiting -the-eu-pm-speech, accessed on 24 January 2017.

Major, John (1999) *The Autobiography* (London: HarperCollins Publishers).

Nelsen, Brent F. and Alexander C-G. Stubb (eds) (1994) *The European Union – Readings on the Theory and Practice of European Integration* (Boulder, CO: Lynne Rienner Publishers, Inc).

Oliver, Craig (2016) 'Brexit Confidential', *The Mail on Sunday*, 25 September, p. 10.

Powell, Charles (1990) 'What the PM learnt about the Germans', minute of a meeting held at Chequers on 24 March, reprinted in *The Independent on Sunday*, 15 July.

R (Miller) v Secretary of State for Exiting the European Union [2016] EWHC 2768, 3 November, available at: www.judiciary.gov.uk/wp-content/uploads/2016/11/r-miller-v-secretary-of-state-for-exiting-eu-amended-2016/122.pdf accessed 3 December 2016.

Reuters (2016) 'Germany, France hit back at Boris Johnson's "baloney" jibe', 23 September, available at: http://uk.reuters.com/article/uk-eu-britain-germany-france-idUKKCN11T1WV, accessed on 25 September 2016.

Salmon, Trevor and Sir William Nicol (1997) eds, *Building European Union – A documentary history and analysis* (Manchester: Manchester University Press).

Seldon, Anthony (1998) *Major: A Political Life* (London: Phoenix, a division of Orion Books Ltd).

Seldon, Anthony (2005) *Blair* (London: The Free Press).

Seldon, Anthony and Peter Snowdon (2016) *Cameron at 10: The Verdict* (London: William Collins, updated paperback edition).

Shonfield, Andrew (1973) *Europe: Journey to an Unknown Destination* (London: Penguin Books).

Smith, Julie (1999) 'The 1975 Referendum', *Journal of European Integration History*, Vol. 5, No. 1, pp. 41–56.

Smith, Julie (2015) 'Europe: The Coalition's Poisoned Chalice' in Anthony Seldon and Mike Finn, eds, *The Coalition Effect, 2010-15* (Cambridge: Cambridge University Press), pp. 372–398.

Smith, Julie (2016) 'David Cameron's EU renegotiation and referendum pledge: A case of déjà vu?', *British Politics*, Vol. 11, No. 3, Sept., pp. 324–46.

Smith, Julie (2016a) 'The United Kingdom' in Donatella Viola, ed., *Routledge Handbook of European Elections* (Abingdon: Routledge).

Smith, Julie (forthcoming) 'National Parliaments and the European Union: A View from Westminster', in Davor Jancic, ed., *National Parliaments after the Lisbon Treaty and the Euro Crisis: Resilience or Resignation?* (Oxford: Oxford University Press).

Spence, David (1991) 'Enlargement without Accession: the EC's Response to German unification', *RIIA Discussion Paper 36* (London: RIIA).

Spicer, Michael (1992) *A Treaty Too Far – A New Policy for Europe* (London: Fourth Estate Ltd).

Stuart, Gisela (2002) 'Convention on the Future of Europe: What is at stake for national parliaments?' *European Essay No. 23* (London: Federal Trust for Education and Research).

Stuart, Gisela (2016) 'I knew the EU had abandoned subsidiarity', *The Tablet*, 18 June, p. 6.

Sunday Times (2016) 'Boris: my case for Britain to stay in Europe', 16 October, p. 1.

Supreme Court (2017) Press Summary R (on the application of Miller and another) (Respondents) v Secretary of State for Exiting the European Union (Appellant), 24 January, available at https://www.supremecourt.uk/cases/docs/uksc-2016-0196-press-summary.pdf, accessed on 24 January 2017.

Thatcher, Margaret (1988) Bruges Speech, 20 September, extracts reprinted in Harryvan and van der Harst, eds, op. cit., pp. 242–247.

Thatcher, Margaret (1993) *The Downing Street Years* (New York: HarperCollins).

Thomson, George [Lord Thomson of Monifieth] (1999) 'Journey to an Unknown Destination: the British Arrival in Brussels in 1973', *The 1999 FCO Annual Lecture No. 16* (London: Foreign and Commonwealth Office).

Tusk, Donald (2016) 'Letter by President Donald Tusk to the Members of the European Council on his proposal for a new settlement for the United Kingdom within the European Union', 2 February, available at: www.consilium.europa.eu/en/press/press-releases/2016/02/02-letter-tusk-proposal-new-settlement-uk/, accessed on 2 December 2016.

Van Rompuy, Herman (2012) 'Herman Van Rompuy, President of the European Council: "Respond with Action and Conviction",' *KU Leuven News*, available at: www.kuleuven.be/english/news/2012/herman-van-rompuy-president-of-the-european-council-respond-with-action-and-conviction, accessed on 3 December 2016.

Van Zeeland, Paul (1948) cited in *Europe Unites – The Hague Congress and After* (London: Hollis and Carter, 1949).

Vanhoonacker, Sophie (1994) 'Introduction: From Maastricht to Karlsruhe: the Long Road to Ratification' in Finn Laursen and Sophie Vanhoonacker, eds, *The Ratification of the Maastricht Treaty: Issues, Debates and Future Implications* (Dordrecht, the Netherlands: Martinus Nijhoff), pp. 3–15.

Vine, Sarah (2016) 'Gosh I suppose I better get up ... ', *The Daily Mail*, 29 June, available at: www.dailymail.co.uk/news/article-3665146/SARAH-VINE-Victory-vitriol-craziest-days-life.html, accessed on 3 November 2016.

Wallace, William and Julie Smith (1995) 'Democracy versus Technocracy – the Problem of Popular Consent' in *West European Politics*, Vol. 18, No. 3, pp. 137–157.

Walters, Simon (2016) 'How Theresa Torpedoed PM Cameron', *The Mail on Sunday*, 25 September.

References

Waterfield, Bruno (2016) 'Decades of politicians' lies led to Brexit, says Juncker', *The Times*, 16 September, available at: http://www.thetimes.co.uk/edition/news/decades-of-politicians-lies-led-to-brexit-says-juncker-5g67vzqfj, accessed on 17 September 2016.

Watt, Nicholas and Patrick Wintour (2015) 'How immigration came to haunt Labour: the inside story', *The Guardian*, 24 March, available at: https://www.theguardian.com, accessed on 8 January 2017.

Wilson, Harold (1967) 'Statement by Harold Wilson on the United Kingdom's application for membership to the EC' (London, 2 May 1967), available at: www.cvce.eu/content/publication/1999/1/1/680afb40-143e-484b-b430-881db671d1ec/publishable_en.pdf, accessed on 3 December 2016.

Young, John W. (1993) *Britain and European Unity, 1945-1992* (Basingstoke: Macmillan Press Ltd).

Young, Hugo (1998) *This Blessed Plot – Britain and Europe from Churchill to Blair* (London and Basingstoke: Macmillan).

Index

acquis communautaire 17–18, 47
Agence Europe 39
Alexander, Danny 89
Alliance of Liberals and Democrats for Europe (ALDE) 72–3, 75
Amsterdam Treaty (1997) 47, 48
Anelay of St Johns, Baroness 81
Article 50 (of Lisbon Treaty) 19, 99, 105, 108, 109; legal challenges to triggering of 101, 112; triggering of, concerns about 100–103; unprecedented nature of invocation of 2–3
Atomic Energy Community 12, 38, proposals for 11–12

Baker, D., Gamble, A. and Ludlam, S. 6, 41, 42
Balance of EU Competences review 57, 64, 70
BBC News 71; balance of BBC during referendum on EU membership 96
Benn, Tony 21–2
Black Wednesday 41, 53
Blair, Tony 4, 18, 25, 28, 71, 75, 93, 107, 110; leaving the people behind 43, 44–5, 47, 49, 51, 52–6; referendum pledge on Constitutional Treaty 50–54
Bloomberg Speech (Cameron, 2013) 58, 69–70, 76–7, 79, 82–3
Bonde, Jens-Peter 49
Brandt, Willy 17, 24

'Brexit means Brexit' 1–3, 99–100, 104–5; uncertainty and 2
Britain in Europe (BiE) 22
Britain Stronger in Europe (BSE) 6, 88–9
British National Party (BNP) 94
Brown, George 16, 24, 26
Brown, Gordon 46, 53, 95; referendum on European Constitution, attitude to 54–5
Browne, Jeremy 63, 65
Bruges Group 50
Brugmans, Hendrik 9
Bush, George W. 18
Butler, D. and Kitzinger, U. 22

Callaghan, James 20–21, 26, 27, 34
Cameron, David 1, 2, 3, 22, 34, 38, 39, 105, 107, 111; Article 50, plans for 101; battle lines 86–8; Black Wednesday and 53; 'Bloomberg speech' and agenda of (2013) 58, 69–70, 76–7, 79, 82–3; coalition government 57–8, 59–60, 61, 62–3, 67, 68, 69; electoral victory (2015) 52; European Parliament elections (2014), Juncker debacle and 73–4; European Union (EU) negotiations, engagement with 28; gamble (and loss) on EU membership 1–2; media Euroscepticism 51; outcome of referendum 98; referendum, preparations for 79–82; referendum campaigns 88–97; referendum date, decision on 103–4;

referendum pledge 55; reform, renegotiation, referendum ('three Rs'), prospects for 78–9; reform and renegotiation 82–6; reform areas, 'baskets' of 82–3, 84; renegotiation outcome, announcement of 85–6
Carswell, Douglas 62, 66
Cash, Bill [Sir William] 32, 33, 41, 62, 67, 85, 93
Cash, W. 41, 51, 52
Cassis de Dijon ruling (ECJ, 1979) 31
Central and Eastern European (CEE) states 35, accession of 5, 43, 45, 46, 48
Chirac, Jacques 54
Christlich-Demokratische Union Deutschlands (CDU) 59
Churchill, Winston 8, 9–10, 'spheres of influence' 10–11, 14–15
Clark, Alan 51
Clarke, Ken 41
Clegg, Nick 55, 60–61, 67, 68, 69
'co-operation procedure' 32–3
Coalition Government in UK: beginnings of 60–63; Coalition Agreement 63–5; 'Europe' as point of disagreement for 60–61; European Elections (2014), Juncker debacle and 72–5; Fixed-Term Parliaments Act (2011) 65, 104; Multiannual Financial Framework (MFF), EU Budget and 70–72; pledges on Europe of Coalition Agreement 64; 'referendum lock' 64; referendum lock, European Union Act (2011) and 65–9; repatriation of powers, Conservative hopes for 70
Cockfield, Lord [Arthur] 31, 33
Coetzee, Ryan 89, 98
Cold War 8, 17, 43, 44, 45
College of Commissioners 48
Common Agricultural Policy (CAP) 18, 22
Common Assembly 12
Common Fisheries Policy (CFP) 18
Commonwealth 5, 10, 15, 81, 92, 95; UK EEC membership, attitude to 22, 23
Communism in Europe, collapse of 35–7

Congress of Europe, The Hague (1948) 9; national sovereignty, cavalier attitudes towards 9
Conservative Party 1, 2, 3, 5, 7, 25, 27, 30, 34, 36, 37–8, 87, 101, 104, 105; accession terms for EEC 19, 20–21; allies in Europe, lack of 60; Coalition Agreement 63–5; divisions over Europe within 61–2; election victory (1970) 18; Euroscepticism of 5, 56, 57–8, 58–60, 61–3; free movement of workers, pressure for return to 83–4, 84–5; in-out referendum on EU, unequivocal commitment to 78; landmark victory for Thatcher (1983) 27; Maastricht Treaty (1992), 'A Treaty too Far' for 39–40, 41–2; Manifesto for 2014 elections to EP 83; Manifesto for general election (2015) 84; party's campaigns 89–97; repatriation of powers from EU, hopes for 70
Constitutional Treaty (2004) 50, 53, 54–5
Convention on the Future of Europe (2001–2003) 49–50
Cook, Robin 53
Cooper, Andrew 89
Copenhagen criteria on accession standards 47, 95
Corbyn, Jeremy 5, 51, 52, 67, 91–2, 94
Costa v ENEL (ECJ, 1964) 13
Council of Ministers 32, 93; establishment of 13
Court of Justice of the European Union (CJEU) 92–3, 103
courts, role of 92–3
Crosby, Lynton 78, 97

Daily Express 66
Daily Mail 62
Daily Star 22
Daily Telegraph 23, 87
Davis, David 102, 106, 107
De Gaulle, Charles (and Gaullist vision of Europe) 15–16, 17, 31, 34; intergovernmental approach to integration 15

Deighton, Anne 14
Delors, Jacques 25, 31, 33–4, 36, 37, 44
Desmond, Richard 66
Dobbs, Michael 96
Du Cann, Edward 32
Dublin Summit (1980) 29–30
Duffy, Gillian 46, 95
Duncan Smith, Iain 58, 86

economic and monetary union (EMU) 4, 18, 36, 38, 39, 41, 42n2; moves towards 26, 33–5
Eden, Anthony 11
Electoral Commission 80, 88, 91
Elliott, F. 89
Elysée Treaty (1963) 16, 59
Euratom 12, 38
Eurobarometer 93
European Coal and Steel Community (ECSC) 11–12, 13, 24, 38
European Commission 2, 14, 18–19, 27, 30, 33, 50, 72, 73–4, 93, 104, 106; emergence of 12–13
European Communities Act (1972) 19–20, 21–2, 52, 61–2, 64, 65, 99–100, 101
European Communities (EC) 7; economics as driving force for 8; geopolitics as driving force for 8; integration within, beginnings of 7–8; law of, assertion of superiority of 13; renaming of EEC as 38; security as driving force for 8; sovereignty, pooling of 13
European Court of Human Rights (ECHR) 13
European Court of Justice (ECJ) 13, 31, 40, 92–3 (see also Court of Justice of the EU)
European Defence Community (EDC) 11, 12
European Economic Community (EEC) 3; budgetary arrangements (and Thatcher's antipathy towards) 18, 21, 28–9; budgetary contributions, renegotiation of 21; economic success 15, 16–17; establishment of 14; first enlargement (1973) 20; outcome of UK referendum on membership (1975) 23–4; renegotiation of terms of accession 20–21; value added tax (VAT), receipts from 21; Wilson's enthusiasm for 16–17
European Free Trade Association (EFTA) 14, 15, 16
European integration, origins of 7–24; *acquis communautaire* 17–18; applications from UK to join (and Community reactions) 14–17; budget, arrangements for 18; Common Agricultural Policy (CAP) 18, 22; Common Fisheries Policy (CFP) 18; European Political Co-operation (EPC) 18, 31; first enlargement (1973) 20; Hague Summit (1969), change following 17–18; Institutions 12–14; outcome of referendum (1975) 23–4; renegotiation by Labour of terms of membership 20–21; supranationalism, emergence of 12–14; UK en route to Europe 18–20
European Parliament (EP): Conservative Manifesto for 2014 elections to 83; direct elections to 27; powers of 27–8
European Parliamentary Assembly 26; emergence of 12–13
European People's Party (EPP) 37–8, 59–60, 68, 72, 73, 74
European Political Co-operation (EPC) 18, 31
European Referendum Act (2015) 3, 80, 101–2
European Union, Treaty of (TEU) *see* Maastricht Treaty
European Union Act (2011) 57, 65, 67, 68
European Union (EU): access to UK labour market, freedom of 55–6; Amsterdam Treaty (1997) 47; Balance of Competences review 57, 64, 70; budgetary rebate, UK giving up part of 55–6; budgetary and institutional cycles 104; Central and Eastern European (CEE) states, accession of 5, 45, 46; changes on leaving, reflection on

Index

108–10; College of Commissioners 48; Constitutional Treaty (2004) 50, 53, 54–5; Convention on the Future of Europe (2001–2003) 49–50; Copenhagen criteria on accession standards 47, 95; economic and monetary union (EMU) 4, 18, 26, 33–5, 36, 38, 39, 41, 42n2; engagement (or otherwise) of UK political parties with 4–5; enlargement of 44–6; enlargement of, UK determination for 55–6; European Elections (2014) in UK, Juncker debacle and 72–5; European 'project,' engagement with 1, 7; 'ever-closer union,' Maastricht Treaty and 39; expansion of, UK support for 44–5; free movement, UK support for 45–6; immigration from, issue of 46; key episodes in relationship with UK 4–6; Laeken Declaration (2001) 48; Lisbon Treaty (2007) 54–5, 56; media, political debate and 4, 5; Nice Treaty (2001) 48; reform and renegotiation, attempts at 82–6; relationship between UK and, strained nature (and problems) of 3–4; Scottish independence referendum and 77; Single European Act (1986) 5, 25, 30–35; Structural Funds 45; themes in UK relationship with 5; VAT receipts 45; withdrawal negotiations, timing of 103–4

Euroscepticism 30, 34, 51–2, 66, 78, 110; concept of 24n1; Conservative Party scepticism 5, 56, 57–8, 58–60, 61–3; drivers of 6; media Euroscepticism 1, 51

Evening Standard 70

Exchange Rate Mechanism (ERM) 26, 34, 36–7

Farage, Nigel 78
federalism, British resistance to 9–10
Fenton, Siobhan 102
Field, Mark 67
Financial Times 33
Fixed-Term Parliaments Act (2011) 65, 104

Fontainebleau European Council (1984) 30
Foreign and Commonwealth Office (FCO) 29, 68, 106–7
Forster, Anthony 41
Forsyth of Drumlean, Lord [Michael] 29, 41
Fox, Liam 106, 108
Franco-German Treaty on Friendship and Reconciliation (1963) see Elysée Treaty
French Presidential elections (2017) 82
functional integration 10

George, Stephen 3, 7, 15
Germany: Federal elections (autumn, 2017) 82; unification of 35–7
Giscard d'Estaing, Valéry 26, 28, 49, 50, 55
Goldsmith, Sir James 42, 50–51
Gove, Michael 1, 86, 89, 94, 98
Gray, J. and Lomas, M. 101
Grayling, Chris 86
Great Repeal Act, proposal for 100
Green, Damian 89
Green Party (in Europe and UK) 72, 73, 80, 90

Hague, William 58, 59, 61
Hague Summit (1969) 17–18, 38; politics of treaty reform 26
Hain, Peter 50
Hammond, Philip 80, 108
Harper, John L. 8
Heath, Edward 5, 7, 18–20, 23, 28, 37
Higgins, Stuart 51
Hill, Jonathan 109
Hitler, Adolf 36
Hollande, François 104
Holloway, Adam 67
Howard, Michael 46, 58–9, 83–4, 94
Howe, Geoffrey 36–7
Huhne, Chris 65
Hurd, Douglas 39

intergovernmental conferences (IGCs) 34, 38, 47, 49, 54
International Monetary Fund (IMF) 21

James, Diane 105
Jenkin, Bernard 40, 62, 67, 85, 111
Jenkins, Roy 26, 27
Johnson, Alan 91
Johnson, Boris 1, 87, 89, 93, 98, 106
Johnson, S. 93
Juncker, Jean-Claude 54, 58, 60, 100, 109–10; European Parliamentary elections (2014) 72–5

Kavanagh, Trevor 51
Kennedy, John F. 15
Kerr of Kinlochard, Lord [John O.] 49
Khan, Sadiq 92
King, Julian 109
Kinnock, Glenys 97
Kinnock, Neil 97
Kinnock, Stephen 97
Kohl, Helmut 35, 36, 38

Labour Party 5, 7, 24, 26, 27, 30, 40, 44–6, 47, 49, 51, 56, 58, 67, 69, 71–2, 105; accession terms for EEC 18–19; Labour government in Britain, concerns of (1948) 10–11; media, Blair and 53; New Labour success (and pro-EU stance) 52–3; opposition to EEC (1980s) 34; party's campaigns 89–97; renegotiation of terms of EEC membership 20–21; Wilson's enthusiasm for EEC 16–17, 25
Laeken Declaration (2001) 48
Lamont, Norman 26, 39, 92–3; Black Wednesday and 53
Lawson, Dominic 35–6
Lawson, Nigel 36
Le Pen, Marine 104
Leave campaign (referendum on EU membership) 1, 5, 30, 49, 56, 58, 61, 67, 80, 84, 87–8, 98; parties' campaigns 90–92; Vote Leave 1, 84, 86, 88, 90, 91, 92–7, 101, 105–6, 107, 108
Liberal Democrats 4–5, 51, 55, 57, 62, 72–3, 77–8, 80, 105; Coalition Agreement 63–5; EU referendum campaign 89, 90–92; formation of 75n1; free movement of people, attitude towards 93–4; party's campaigns 89–97; pro-Europeanism of 60–61, 63, 67; *see also* Coalition Government in UK
Liddle, Roger 105
Lisbon Treaty (2007) 54–5, 56

Maastricht Treaty (1992) 37–42; 'A Treaty too Far,' Conservative perspectives on 39–40, 41–2; European integration, high point of 44; justice and home affairs (JHA) 38; opposition to 6; ratification of, difficulties of 40–41; McDonnell, John 67
Macmillan, Harold 14–15, 18
Major, John 28, 36, 44, 51, 52, 56, 65, 88, 106; Amsterdam Treaty 47; Convention on Future of Europe 49; Maastricht and 37–42
Mandelson, Peter 89
Mann, Thomas 38
Marr, Andrew 68
Marshall Aid 8
Mauriac, François 8, 38
May, Theresa 1, 2, 3, 99–100, 101, 103; Brexit under, options for 104–8
media: EU referendum campaign 91–2, 93, 97; media Euroscepticism 1, 24, 51; media scrutiny 60; political debate and 4, 5, 13, 22–3, 27, 53. 74; print media 45, 51, 66, 87; in Scottish referendum 77–8
membership of EU, continuity of issues of 110–11
Merkel, Angela 54, 59–60, 74, 75, 100–101, 104
Messina negotiations (1955) 12
Miliband, Ed 67
Monnet, Jean 10, 11, 15
Moore, Charles 23
Moore, Richard 23, 24n2
Multiannual Financial Framework (MFF) 45, 70–72, 75, 84, 104
Murdoch, Rupert 51, 52

National Health Service (NHS) 29; commitment to, concerns about 96
National Referendum Campaign (NRC, 1975) 22–3

national sovereignty 9
Neill, Bob 75n4
New Labour success (and pro-Europen stance) 52–3
Nice Treaty (2001) 48
North Atlantic Treaty Organization (NATO) 8, 36
Northern Ireland 87
Norway, rejection of EEC membership 19
Nuttall, David 66

Obama, Barack 97
Oliver, Craig 98
Orban, Viktor 74
Organisation for European Economic Cooperation (OEEC) 8
Osborne, George 68

Paris Treaty (1951) 11, 13
Party of European Socialists (PES) 72, 73, 75
Patel, Priti 86
Pöhl, Karl Otto 36
Political Parties, Elections and Referendums Act 2000 (PPERA) 79–80
politics of treaty reform 25–42; budgetary arrangements, Thatcher's antipathy towards 28–9; *Cassis de Dijon* ruling (ECJ, 1979) 31; 'cooperation procedure' 32–3; Communism in Europe, collapse of 35–7; contribution problem, Thatcher and price of membership 28–30; Dublin Summit (1980) 29–30; economic and monetary union (EMU), moves towards 26, 33–5; enthusiasm for Europe, lack of 26–8; Euratom 38; European Community, renaming of EEC as 38; European Parliament (EP), direct elections to 27; European Parliament (EP), powers of 27–8; European People's Party (EPP) 37–8, 59–60, 68, 72, 73, 74; 'ever-closer union,' Maastricht Treaty and 39; Exchange Rate Mechanism (ERM) 26, 34, 36–7; Fontainebleau European Council (1984) 30; German unification 35–7; Hague Summit (1969), change following 26; intergovernmental conferences (IGCs) 34, 38, 47, 49, 54; justice and home affairs (JHA), Maastricht Treaty (1992) 37–42; qualified majority voting (QMV) 31–2, 33, 44, 50, 56; ramifications of Single European Act (1986), far-reaching nature of 33–4; ratification of Single European Act (1986) 32; Single European Act (1986) 25, 30–35; sovereignty, Single European Act (1986) and loss of 31–2; Werner Report (1970) 26, 34, 42n2
Pompidou, Georges 17, 18, 19
Powell, Enoch 22, 35, 36
Project Fear 77–8, 90, 97, 111
Putin, Vladimir 97

qualified majority voting (QMV) 31–2, 33, 44, 50, 56
Question Time (BBC TV) 105

R (Miller) v Secretary of State for Exiting the European Union (November, 2016) 102–3
Reckless, Mark 62, 66, 71–2
Redwood, John 62, 67
Rees-Mogg, Jacob 62, 85
referendum lock, European Union Act (2011) and 64, 65–9
referendum on EU membership 1, 2, 88–98; balance of BBC during 96; battle lines, drawing of 86–7; campaigns 89; commitment to NHS, concerns about 96; cost of EU membership, concerns about 96; courts, role of 92–3; democratic accountability, concerns about 92–3; enlargement of EU, fears about 96; free movement of people, concerns about 93–6; objective information on EU exit, Lords' efforts on 81–2; outcome 98; parties' campaigns 90–92; preparations for 79–82; Project Fear 77–8, 90, 97, 111; reform and renegotiation, attempts at 82–6; sovereignty, concerns about 93; Vote Leave 1, 84, 86, 88, 90, 91, 92–7, 101, 106

Referendum Party 52–3
Rehn, Olli 73
Reinfeldt, Fredrik 74
Remain campaign (referendum on EU membership) 4, 6, 52, 55–6, 61, 80, 87, 89, 96, 103, 105; parties' campaigns 90–92
Ridley, Nicholas 35–6
Rome, Treaties of (1957) 12, 13, 14, 16; Article 237 in original version 14, 15; freedoms under 31
Roper, John 19
Rose of Monewden, Lord [Stuart] 88–9
Rutte, Mark 74

Sainsbury of Turville, Lord [David J.] 89
Salisbury Convention 2–3, 6n1
Salmon, T. and Nicol, W. 11, 16
Schmidt, Helmut 21, 26
Schulz, Martin 72, 73
Schuman, Robert 9, 10, 15
Schuman Declaration (1950) 9, 10, 11
Scottish National Party (SNP) 3, 77, 78, 92
Seldon, Anthony 51, 53
Shonfield, Andrew 3, 111
Single European Act (1986) 5, 13, 30, 31–2, 37, 41–2, 43, 44, 54, 64; politics of treaty reform 25, 30–35; ramifications of, far-reaching nature of 33–4; ratification of 32
Sked, Alan 42
Smith, Julie 22, 23, 57, 98n1
sovereignty: concerns about, referendum campaign and 93; national sovereignty 9; Single European Act (1986) and loss of 31–2
Soviet Union 8
Spectator 22, 35
Spence, David 36
Spicer, Michael 39
Steed, Michael 75n2
Stewart, Michael 16
Straw, Jack 54
Structural Funds 45
Stuart, Gisela 49–50, 93
Sturgeon, Nicola 103

Suez Crisis (1956) 14–15
Sun 51
Sunday Times 87
supranationalism, emergence of 12–14
Supreme Court ruling 112

Thatcher, Margaret 4, 71, 75, 97, 107; Bruges Speech (1988) 34; concerns on price of EEC membership 28–30; landmark victory for (1983) 27; leaving the people behind 43, 44, 45, 50, 54, 56; treaty reform, money, power and politics of 25, 27, 28–32, 33, 34, 35–7, 39, 41–2, 42n3
Thomson of Monifieth, Lord [George] 19
Thorning-Schmidt, Helle 97
Times 51, 97
Today Programme (BBC Radio 4) 97
Treaty establishing a Constitution for Europe (TCE) *see* Constitutional Treaty
Turkey, EU membership for 95–6
Tusk, Donald 79, 82, 84

UK Independence Party (UKIP) 4, 5, 42, 46, 51–2, 56, 105; Conservatives in coalition and 58, 61, 62, 66, 73; party's campaigns 89–97; referendum and 77, 78, 80, 83, 94
United Kingdom (UK): access to labour market, freedom of 55–6; applications to join Community from (and Community reactions) 14–17; awkward partnership with Europe 24; Backbench Business Committee of House of Commons 66; budgetary rebate, giving up part of 55–6; cost of EU membership, concerns about 96; democratic accountability, concerns about 92–3; EEC terms of accession, renegotiation of 20–21; Electoral Commission 80, 88, 91; electoral dynamics of, 'Europe' in 51–2; en route to Europe 18–20; engagement (or otherwise) of political parties with EU 4–5;

enlargement of, EU determination for 55–6; enthusiasm for Europe, lack of 26–8; 'Europe' as point of disagreement for Coalition Government in 60–61; expansion of EU, support for 44–5; fears about enlargement of EU 96; free movement of people, concerns about 93–6; free movement of people, support for 45–6; Great Repeal Act, proposal for 100; immigration from EU, issue of 46; key episodes in relationship with EU 4–6; pledges on Europe of Coalition Agreement 64; referendum on EEC membership (1975) 21–4; relationship between EU and, strained nature (and problems) of 3–4; repatriation of powers from EU, Conservative hopes for 70; Royal Prerogative in 101, 103; Second World War, experiences before and after 8; withdrawal negotiations, timing of 103–4; *see also* Coalition Government in UK

United States 8, 9, 10, 18, 30; UK associations with, de Gaulle's fears of 15–16

value added tax (VAT), receipts from 21, 30, 45
Van Gend en Loos case (1963) 13
Van Rompuy, Herman 67
Van Zeeland, Paul 9
Vanhoonacker, Sophie 40
Verhofstadt, Guy 72–3
Villiers, Theresa 86, 87
Vine, Sarah 98
Vote Leave 1, 84, 86, 88, 90, 91, 92–7, 101, 106

Wallace, W. and Smith, J. 9
Walters, Alan 36–7
Walters, S. 87
Waterfield, Bruno 110
Watt, N. and Wintour, P. 46
Welle, Klaus 59
Werner Report (1970) 26, 34, 42n2
Western European Union (WEU) 11
Wharton, James 69–70
Whittingdale, John 86
Wilson, Harold 7, 16–17, 18, 20, 21, 25, 26, 28, 85; enthusiasm for EEC 16–17

Young, Hugo 12, 16, 18, 21